# An 'American' MK

Behind the scenes in the 19th Knesset

Rabbi Dov Lipman

*Trafford rev. 02/03/2016*

 **Trafford**
PUBLISHING®  www.trafford.com
**North America & international**
toll-free: 1 888 232 4444 (USA & Canada)
fax: 812 355 4082

# CONTENTS

# PREFACE
## By MK Yair Lapid

Dov Lipman is 40 years younger than my father, skinnier by at least 50 kilo, and 10 centimeters shorter. In addition, he is an Orthodox rabbi who moved from Maryland to Bet Shemesh while my father was a total atheist who moved from the Budapest ghetto to Tel Aviv.

And despite all this, Dov reminds me of my father!

Why?

Because in each of their life stories strongly beats the same basic experience - migration.

A person doesn't cease to be a migrant on the day that he descends from the airplane or from the ship. Just the opposite - that is the day on which his migration experience begins and, for many, it never ends.

There are some people whose migration experience translates for them into being a foreigner forever and into an eternal attempt to broker between cultures and languages. With Dov, just like with my father, it translated into a deep, strong connection with the new homeland. Because a true migrant is a "convert" and converts as the idiom goes, are always holier than the pope. Israel is not a place where Dov Lipman lives. It is the basic idea from which he functions. The state, for him, is something personal.

And perhaps, because of this, he was such a superb member of Knesset. Because his Knesset activity did not separate between the personal and the national for even one moment.

It was the opposite of Louis XIV's statement - with Dov the "I" is the state. He was a Knesset member in his totality because all existence in the rest of his life became a part of it. He was a rabbi and an MK, a father and an MK, a husband and an MK. All that we who were born in Israel view as part of the theater of politics - speeches in the plenum, interrupting other speakers, committee work - was for him a way to express something deep about his life.

I recently came across a statement from a man named Harris who explained with wondrous preciseness the difference between a patriot and a nationalist: "A patriot," he said, "is a person who praises his country's strengths and tries to correct its weaknesses. A nationalist is someone who praises his country's strengths and tries to conceal its weaknesses."

If this is the criteria, Dov Lipman is among the greatest patriots that I have ever met. Because every injustice, every failure, every crack in the life of the state becomes personal for him. He doesn't sleep, he cries, he fights. He was the first to arrive at the Knesset in the morning and the last to leave because he believed - and still believes - that his role is to fix the state which he chose, every day anew.

This book gives the reader a glimpse of the patriotism, passion, and professionalism which Dov brought to the 19th Knesset and will hopefully bring to many more terms in the Knesset.

# INTRODUCTION

*"Mitchayev Ani"* - *"I obligate myself."*

With those words, life changed. I was suddenly a member of the Israeli Knesset. Less than ten years after moving to Israel from the United States, I was given a mandate to try to make our country better, and blessed with the honor to serve in the parliament of the Jewish state, the institution that is the greatest expression of our independence and rebirth as a nation in our biblical homeland.

As I stood in that hallowed chamber on a beautiful Jerusalem day in January 2013, many things were running through my mind. First and foremost, I thought about the approximately 200,000 English-speakers living in Israel who had not had representation in the Knesset in close to three decades. I was determined to represent their communal and individual needs whether they voted for my political party or not.

I thought about tens of thousands of ultra-Orthodox young men looking for leadership that would give them the ability to receive a general education, enter the workforce, and serve the country – all without giving up on their belief system and traditions and, even more importantly, without being made to feel like they were turning their backs on their upbringing. I committed myself to doing everything possible to help them.

I thought about hundreds of thousands of secular Israelis, including many in my hometown of Bet Shemesh, who feel alienated from Israel's religious establishment because of the extreme approach which the ultra-Orthodox political parties instituted over the course of the past few decades.

Finally, I thought about how many, if not most, Israeli citizens viewed the position of Knesset member with cynicism, and at times, even disdain because of corruption, scandals and a lack of accountability and professionalism. I committed myself to learning this new trade as quickly as possible, and to being the best Knesset member possible on all levels.

This book gives insight into the experience of my two years as a member of the 19th Knesset. Every morning, as the car turned the corner and I saw that majestic building before my eyes, I looked skyward and thanked God for giving me the opportunity to serve in this special role.

I was living a dream.

# ACKNOWLEDGEMENTS

The list of thank you's for this book is way too long to put into print. I have been blessed with hundreds of family members, friends, teachers and colleagues who played a role in my reaching the Knesset and I will have to settle for a very general thank you to all of you.

A special thank you goes to Shalom Lerner who gave me my introduction to public life when he accepted me as a volunteer assistant when he served as deputy mayor of Bet Shemesh. I thank MK Yair Lapid and all of my colleagues, friends and supporters in the Yesh Atid party for welcoming me into the Yesh Atid. I also thank MK Lapid for the beautiful preface he wrote for this book. Similarly, I thank Knesset Speaker MK Yuli Edelstein for his letter of support for this book and for the special relationship we shared in the Knesset. Alisa Coleman and Benjy Goldberg, my advisors and assistants, were partners in all that I did in the 19th Knesset and my thanks to them knows no bounds. I thank P'nina Seplowitz, executive director of American Friends of Yesh Atid, for the hours she dedicated to assisting me with my visits to Jewish communities throughout North America. Elli Wohlgelernter became a good friend and confidant during the 19th Knesset and I thank him for his friendship and for editing this book.

Thank you to Dr. Larry and Wendy Platt, Stuart and Evie Steinberg, and Ken and Nira Abramowitz for their friendship and for sponsoring the book. I also thank my cousin Barbara Maybruch and my mother and her husband, Leah and Allen Zeiger, for their meaningful dedications. The staff at Trafford publishing helped produce a beautiful book and I thank them for their professionalism.

I was blessed to dance with all four of my grandparents at my wedding and everyone of them had a major impact in my life. I thank Zaidy, Rev. Abraham Kleinman, and Grammy and Grandpa, Marvin and Blanche Lipman, for being such wonderful role models and I miss them terribly. I thank God that Bubby, Ethel Kleinman, is alive and healthy.

Her visit to the Knesset was one of the highlights of my term in office. I thank her for being such an inspiration and for her love, guidance and support. May God grant her many more years of good health to enjoy her children, grandchildren, great-grandchildren and her newborn great-great-grandchild.

My parents raised me and my sisters to think about how we can help others and impact the broader community. I miss my father, Ron Lipman, of blessed memory, and think about him throughout my day. It is hard to believe that I was not able to share all the experiences in this book with him but he has been with me every step of the way. While in the Knesset I would constantly ask myself "What would Daddy do?" or "What would Daddy advise me to do?" I am thrilled that my mother, Leah Lipman Zeiger, and her husband, Dr. Allen Zeiger, spend much of their time in Israel and have been able to share in my experiences. I thank them for their constant support and thank my mother for editing this book. I thank my in laws, Rabbi Moshe and Cheryl Abramowitz, for their support from across the ocean.

No one can succeed in politics without a strong family unit and I am so thankful for my wife, Dena, and our wonderful children – Shlomo, Devora, Chaya and Zahava. All of you push and encourage me as we try to make the world a better place together. But I am even more thankful for the fun times which we share. No matter how busy or difficult a day may be, I know that I will come home to your smiles and I treasure that.

God has been so good to me and I thank him for giving me the opportunity to live and raise my family in Israel, and to play an active role in trying to improve our special country. Any success that I have is only through His grace and blessing. I hope and pray that He provide me with many more opportunities to positively impact Israel and that we be blessed with the peace and redemption speedily in our days.

Dov Lipman
Jerusalem
4 Shevat 5776
January 14, 2016

# DEDICATION

*In memory of our parents who taught us the importance of leadership in Klal Yisrael. In honor of our children and grandchildren who are following this path, and in honor of Rabbi Dov Lipman who has clearly dedicated himself to Torah V'avoda and service to Medinat Yisrael. And in honor of all those that have, will or are serving in the IDF especially the Lone Soldiers. Finally in memory of all the soldiers in the IDF who lost their lives protecting and defending the State of Israel.*

*Wendy and Larry Platt*

*Los Angeles California*

\*\*\*\*\*\*\*\*\*\*\*\*\*\*\*\*\*\*\*\*\*\*\*\*\*\*\*\*\*\*\*\*\*\*\*\*\*\*\*\*\*\*\*\*\*\*\*\*\*\*\*\*\*\*\*\*\*\*\*\*\*\*\*\*\*\*\*\*\*\*

# DEDICATION

*Compliments of*

*Ken and Nira Abramowitz*

\*\*\*\*\*\*\*\*\*\*\*\*\*\*\*\*\*\*\*\*\*\*\*\*\*\*\*\*\*\*\*\*\*\*\*\*\*\*\*\*\*\*\*\*\*\*\*\*\*\*\*\*\*\*\*\*\*\*\*\*\*\*\*\*\*\*\*\*\*\*

# DEDICATION

*In honor of Mrs. Ethel Kleinman, the author's Bubby*

*Bubby is a force of nature who sets the tone for our entire family. Her strong will and determination enabled her to survive Auschwitz and endure great pain and suffering, both physical and emotional, throughout her life. Her sense of humor and street smarts saw her through many trials and tribulations. Her influence on all of us is boundless. Bubby, together with her beloved husband, Zaidy Avrohom Aizik Kleinman, a"h, poured the foundation upon which the family lived a life dedicated to improving the lot of all Jews. May she continue to be an inspiration to the entire family.*

*Leah and Allen Zeiger*

\*\*\*\*\*\*\*\*\*\*\*\*\*\*\*\*\*\*\*\*\*\*\*\*\*\*\*\*\*\*\*\*\*\*\*\*\*\*\*\*\*\*\*\*\*\*\*\*\*\*\*\*\*\*\*\*\*\*\*\*\*\*\*\*\*\*\*\*\*\*

\*\*\*\*\*\*\*\*\*\*\*\*\*\*\*\*\*\*\*\*\*\*\*\*\*\*\*\*\*\*\*\*\*\*\*\*\*\*\*\*\*\*\*\*\*\*\*\*\*\*\*\*\*\*\*\*\*\*\*\*\*\*\*\*\*

# DEDICATION

*In loving memory of our son and fallen soldier*

*Sgt. Max Steinberg*

*Stuart and Evie Steinberg*

\*\*\*\*\*\*\*\*\*\*\*\*\*\*\*\*\*\*\*\*\*\*\*\*\*\*\*\*\*\*\*\*\*\*\*\*\*\*\*\*\*\*\*\*\*\*\*\*\*\*\*\*\*\*\*\*\*\*\*\*\*\*\*\*\*

# DEDICATION

*In loving memory of Rabbi Joseph Fischman*

**הרב חיים יוסף בן הרב אלימלך פישמן, זצ״ל**

*Great-uncle of the author who had a love for Israel
and dedicated his life to the Jewish people*

*From his daughter Barbara Maybruch*

\*\*\*\*\*\*\*\*\*\*\*\*\*\*\*\*\*\*\*\*\*\*\*\*\*\*\*\*\*\*\*\*\*\*\*\*\*\*\*\*\*\*\*\*\*\*\*\*\*\*\*\*\*\*\*\*\*\*\*\*\*\*\*\*\*

# HOW IT ALL BEGAN

Stepping off the El Al airplane on July 14, 2004, as a new immigrant to Israel, the idea of serving in the Knesset was not on my radar screen. I was an educator, and was looking forward to teaching in post-high school gap year programs for English-speaking students, with the hope of strengthening their connection to Israel and Judaism before they begin university. I moved to the city of Bet Shemesh with my wife and four children, and quickly learned that while we moved to a remarkable state – only 56 years old at the time – disagreements and tensions between different populations within Israel were very much alive and well. The population of Bet Shemesh - a city of 80,000 residents at the time - included residents who were ultra-Orthodox, secular, traditional and religious Zionists from a blend of native Israelis and immigrants from Russia, Ethiopia, France and English-speaking countries. It was truly a microcosm of Israeli society.

One night several months after our move, I heard a commotion near our apartment building. I went outside and saw three police cars on the corner. Fearing some kind of a terror threat, I asked one of the policemen what was going on. He told me to run away as fast as I could. Before I had a chance to ask why, a hailstorm of rocks rained down on us and I was hit in the leg by a rock, causing it to bleed. The entire incident revolved around a demonstration by ultra-Orthodox extremists against what they viewed as the desecration of old Jewish graves in the city of Yaffo. In protest, they blocked my street in Bet Shemesh. The police had arrived in order to clear the street and some of the protestors stoned the police. I was stunned to discover that there were no newspaper headlines reporting this incident about Jews stoning fellow Jews. Apparently, this was simply not considered an unusual, and thus newsworthy, occurrence in our state.

Over time, the incidents of religious extremism became more and more regular – usually targeting women. One morning we woke up to see bright yellow signs on walls throughout our neighborhood declaring: "It is forbidden for women to walk on these streets in clothing deemed immodest." I could not believe that anyone had the nerve to post signs which made these demands on residents of a city with such a mixed population. At the time, I had no political connections and did not know where to turn for help. I felt that I could not live with offensive signs of this sort posted in my neighborhood, so I went to a hardware store, bought spray paint, woke up in middle of the night and spray painted over the offensive messages. When replacement signs were posted, I recruited a team of spray painters to make sure that no sign lasted a day without being covered over. At a certain point, the cost of the spray paint became prohibitive so I started covering just the last two words on the signs. The signs then read: "It is forbidden for women to walk on these streets in clothing." The signs stopped appearing.

The problems increased and the resulting tensions bothered me to the core. I decided that I would try to get involved in the local leadership and attempt to make a difference. People told me that there was a Deputy Mayor of Bet Shemesh, Shalom Lerner, who spoke English. I was extremely nervous when I called his office to ask for a meeting and even more nervous when I walked through the doors of City Hall to meet with him. I asked Shalom if there was any way that I could be of assistance. He was shocked. He told me that his meetings with city residents are always from people who want him to do something for them or who want to complain. He could not believe that someone was offering to help. Shalom accepted my offer and I began helping him with various projects including helping to arrange the then-popular Bet Shemesh festival which I saw as a potentially unifying event for a city in need of healing and harmony.

I was introduced to the dirtiness of Israeli politics when Shalom asked me to work on a project as part of the portfolio for tourism in the city. Tourism doesn't exist in Bet Shemesh despite tremendous potential as a Biblical city. This is the area where Samson roamed at Nachal Sorek at the city's northern edge, and the battlefield of David and Goliath sits in the Valley of Elah at the city's southern edge. Shalom had an idea to build an interactive museum about Biblical heroes and he tasked me with exploring the possibility of finding interested donors for this project. I made contact with some people in the United States and found that there was interest in donating towards this effort. I met with the holders of privately owned land at the southern entrance to the city – the perfect location from which shuttles could bus people to the actual sites where the Biblical events took place. The plans reached the point where Shalom needed a green light from the Mayor to take it to the next step. He met with the Likud Mayor who quickly shot down the idea. There was no justification for the negative response, nor did he offer an explanation. It was clear that with the 2008 municipal elections approaching and Shalom, as deputy mayor, posing a possible threat in those elections, the mayor was not going to let Shalom succeed in anything, even if it was for the benefit of the city. This was a real eye opener for me, but a great experience and lesson for my future political journey.

Sure enough, Shalom did run in the 2008 elections and I was by his side every step of the way as one of his campaign managers. My goal was simple: the city should be in the hands of an honest and decent leader who would provide services to all the city's residents and create an atmosphere of unity and harmony with zero tolerance for acts of religious extremism. Unfortunately, we lost those elections and the city fell prey to even more extremist hands. We dealt with more and more outrageous acts and all of my e-mails to members of Knesset and ministers went unanswered. At the height of our local struggles, with extremists coming to the street almost daily to verbally assault young girls on their way home from school, I came to understand that many ministers did not want to get involved because this could cause issues in their coalition with the ultra-Orthodox parties. I was sick that any "leaders" would have these considerations while little girls were being tormented on the streets of my city.

*At a demonstration in Bet Shemesh*

I made the decision to get involved in national politics so there could be a voice of reason, tolerance, and unity from the religious side. I also wanted to have influence on the ultra-Orthodox community. I reflected a lot about the extremism which I saw in Bet Shemesh and came to the conclusion that the extremism was a result of the isolation of the community. The ideology of not serving in the army, not entering the work force and not learning general studies created a barrier between the ultra-Orthodox community and the rest of Israeli society, and the minimal interaction, at best, between the two bred an extremely negative perspective towards broader Israel. That is what led to the extremism, so there needed to be a political voice seeking change in that community.

My first step was to reach out to former MK Rabbi Haim Amsalem from the Shas party, who started a political movement called Am Shalem – the complete nation – which sought the inclusion of the ultra-Orthodox into the army and the workforce, a more moderate approach to conversions while remaining within the framework of Jewish law, and breaking down barriers between populations. I was thrilled when his office replied to e-mail offering to get involved and I quickly became part of his inner circle.

*Speaking in the USA with then MK Rabbi Haim Amsalem*

In the end, I and other Am Shalem activists left the movement due to various internal conflicts and ideological issues, but the experience being involved with a high-level figure and an important movement was invaluable.

Yair Lapid was the most popular television personality in Israel at the time but I had no exposure to him. All I had heard about Yair was negative including that he was "anti Torah," "anti- religion," and "anti the ultra-Orthodox." A friend sent me a link to a speech which Yair gave to a group of ultra-Orthodox young men at Kiryat Ono shortly before he announced that he was entering politics. I was blown away. In that speech I saw a person who was anything but anti-religious or anti-ultra-Orthodox. On the contrary! He was a leader with a vision for unity and working together. He expressed that he and the rest of the secular population accepted that God, Torah study and religious observance were an integral part of the State of Israel. All he asked from the ultra-Orthodox population was that they share in the responsibility of running the state and refrain from forcing their beliefs on the secular population. As I watched Yair speak, I envisioned a hand coming out from the secular side seeking to work together with the religious community. I wanted to be one of the people who grabbed that extended hand.

Getting in touch with Yair Lapid was not easy. Using connections in the media which I developed during our battles in Bet Shemesh, and writing an email to a generic e-mail address - "lapidteam@gmail.com" - I managed to obtain a meeting with one of the handful of volunteers on Yair's team. The meeting took place in a rented back room of a Tel Aviv law office. I explained to the volunteer why I, as an Orthodox rabbi, wanted to be involved in the developing, new political party. She asked me to arrange an event for Lapid in Bet Shemesh. After that we would explore how to best move forward. The event was a huge success, resulting in a meeting with Yair.

*At one of the first events that I arranged for Yair Lapid*

That first meeting with Yair Lapid was very special. We talked about our visions for Israel and about very personal matters. At the end of the meeting, Yair said to me: "Dov, it is amazing. We come from different planets – you, an Orthodox Jew from Silver Spring, Maryland and I, a very secular Jew from aristocratic Tel Aviv. But we agree about 80 percent of the issues. And yet, Israeli society has told us that we should be in different camps, fighting against each other. Let's change that, break down that barrier, and work together. Let's move forward on the 80 percent upon which we agree, and on the remaining 20 percent let's sit around a table and come to compromise and understandings. In the end the country will not look 100 percent the way I may want it to look, nor will it look 100 percent the way you may want it to look. But at least we will have found a way to get along with one another here." I told Yair that his words were music to my ears, and that I wanted to be a part of this movement. We agreed that I would head the Bet Shemesh branch of the new party, called "Yesh Atid" ("there is a future") and I set out to do my part in helping the party achieve success.

At a certain point, the party leadership asked for my resume and I met with some of them as it became clear that they were considering me to fill one of the slots on the party list. In Israel, every party completes a list of 120 candidates for Knesset. The percentage of votes which the party receives determines how many of those candidates enter the 120-member Knesset. A few months before the January 2013 elections, Yair invited me to meet with him at a café near his home in Ramat Aviv in Tel Aviv where he offered me the number 17 slot on the party's Knesset list. At that time, Yesh Atid was polling in single digits and my spot was not even remotely realistic. I told Yair that I accepted the offer with great honor even though it was not realistic at all, but that I looked forward to helping the party from outside the Knesset in its efforts relating to the ultra-Orthodox community and on issues of religion and state.

*A newspaper display of the Yesh Atid candidates*

Yair responded that I did not understand the significance of this offer and that I, just eight and a half years after walking down the steps of that airplane as a new immigrant, would end up as a member of Knesset. I doubted his prediction because of the polls and because of the impossibility of this unlikely scenario playing out for me. I worked hard during the elections conducting parlor meetings, handing out materials and engaging shoppers in malls and taking part in both Hebrew and English debates, never campaigning for my unrealistic spot but sharing the party's platform and vision.

## *The campaign trail*

The night before the elections, I received a phone call from a newspaper telling me that my spot had become realistic according to the exit polls. I immediately went to the Western Wall to pray, as I suddenly found myself on the cusp of potentially being elected to the Knesset. I sent a text message to Yair telling him that I was at the Kotel praying for him, praying for the party and praying for myself. I was number 17 on the list and Boaz Toporovksy was number 18. Yair answered me via text: "Dear Dov, I already closed the deal in terms of you. Now I am working on Toporovsky's spot." On election night, after an intense and challenging election campaign and amidst our celebration over winning 19 seats, Yair grabbed me and said, "I told you so."

*Celebrating election results with fellow newly elected MK's*
*Yael German, Penina Tamanu-Shata, and Rena Frenkel*

# LEARNING THE TRADE

January 22, 2013 is a day I will never forget. Election Day was nothing short of magical. A few months of hard work came to an end at 10:00 p.m. when the exit polls were displayed on three screens in the front of election headquarters. Pandemonium and mass celebration erupted as all three television stations reported that our party, Yesh Atid, had won 19 seats and was to be the second-largest party in the Knesset. Following Yair Lapid's victory speech, the 19 of us gathered in a side room and Yair pointed to the room's windows through which we could see numerous television cameras filming and then to a television screen inside the room showing our meeting live on national television. "Life is not going to be the same for any of us," he said, and that our focus has to be on getting to work.

*Placing my vote in the ballot box on Election Day*

I had two major fears when I woke up the next morning. The first - making sure that my Hebrew was up to par for the Knesset - was one that I would need to confront on my own. The second - learning how to be a successful member of Knesset - was one which I shared with 47 other freshman MK's, including all 19 from our party. Yesh Atid arranged for "Knesset school" – a few very intensive days during which we learned the logistics, the weekly schedule, how a bill becomes a law, the role of the various committees, the importance of "shdulot" which are Knesset lobbies or taskforces and other ways to make use of our position to change the country for the better.

*Enjoying the company of colleagues and good friends Ronen*
*Hoffman and Boaz Toporovsky during a break at "Knesset school*

The weekly schedule struck me as "light" when described on paper. The plenum meets on Mondays and Tuesdays at 4:00 p.m. and on Wednesdays starting at 11:00 a.m. To my surprise, we were told that MK's generally don't appear at the Knesset on Sundays and Thursdays. I remember naively asking why the plenums start so late in the afternoon on Mondays and Tuesdays, and recall not fully understanding the answer that there had to be committee time to prepare for those plenum sessions. I learned very quickly how critical those committee hours were to the success or failure of the plenum sessions. I would also learn how the plenum schedule was anything but "light," and for an MK who takes his job seriously, it is actually quite grueling. We learned the difficult process of passing legislation. All of the presenters, former Knesset members, emphasized that committees and shdulot are where we can really make a difference without the rigorous procedures and obstacles of the legislation process.

The Knesset also held an orientation for the 48 new members. This was my first opportunity to introduce myself to MK's from other parties. I was pleasantly surprised to see how much camaraderie there was among MK's and how friendships crossed all party lines. As an outsider, observing the intense and passionate debates on television, I assumed that there was limited social interaction between MK's of different parties. During the first few minutes of orientation I realized how wrong I was. I met new parliamentarians from across the political spectrum and could immediately identify those who were potential work-mates on a wide range of issues and potential friends on a personal level.

*Cross party camaraderie – with my teammates on the Knesset soccer team:*
*Yaakov Margi (Shas), Tzachi Hanegbi (Likud), Eli ben Dahan (Bayit*
*Yehudi), Hamad Amar (Yisrael Beiteinu), Issawi Frej (Meretz)*

The Knesset staff walked us through the maze of Knesset hallways in an attempt to give us some idea where things were. I must admit that several weeks after the inauguration, I could still be found wandering around trying to get from one place to the other.

The one place we all remembered how to find was the plenum. I vividly recall how we braced ourselves as the guards opened those doors and we were escorted into that hallowed chamber for the first time. It was surreal. I could not believe where I was. I stood near the doorway for a few minutes to take it all in and then found my assigned seat – our names were already there.

*Sitting in my plenum seat for the first time on orientation day*

We did a practice vote, and while soon pressing those buttons became a routine part of my day, that first practice vote with no significance was an awesome experience never to be forgotten.

Once I felt somewhat equipped to deal with my first challenge - knowing what it means to be an MK - I set my sites on my second challenge, one which no other MK shared with me: improving my Hebrew. The first step was to start reading a Hebrew newspaper every day. This enabled me to become more conversant with the "language of the Knesset" - technical terminology that was never part of my lexicon of conversational Hebrew. The Knesset provides MK's with a budget to learn another language. Most MK's use it for English, some for Russian, and others for Arabic. I was the only one who used this budget for Hebrew. I spent two hours a week with my tutor, Nadav, who critiqued my Hebrew interviews and speeches from the previous week, taught me some of the more complex elements of grammar which I had not yet mastered and taught me words related to the more technical side of my Knesset work. These sessions worked wonders for me, giving me increased confidence to conquer the fear of functioning in Hebrew in the public sphere.

A few days before the inauguration, I received a letter from the Knesset informing me that according to Israeli law, I was required to renounce my United States citizenship prior to the inauguration. I arranged to go to the embassy at a time when it was closed to the public in order to avoid having to renounce my American citizenship with undue attention. After signing a document and paying the fee, I was called to appear before a clerk who was sitting behind a glass. She asked me to raise my right hand and repeat after her. I asked, "I have to say this?" She said yes. With tears in my eyes I formally renounced my United States citizenship "without coercion."

The emotion, which made it difficult for me to speak, came from a feeling of slapping America in the face. This is the country which gave my father's side of the family safe haven from pogroms in Russia in the late 19th century and welcomed my mother's family after the Holocaust. Growing up in the United States I had every opportunity to live as an Orthodox Jew without ever experiencing anti-Semitism. My father of blessed memory was a judge in the Federal government and the American flag flew proudly outside our home 365 days a year. Therefore, saying those words was extremely difficult. I felt so bad about it that I sat down and wrote a letter, "Thank You America," and asked Ambassador Dan Shapiro to hand it to President Obama next time he saw him. I needed to do something to assuage my guilt. A few short hours later, it struck me with great pride that my nationality was now 100 percent Israeli.

Following Inauguration Day, I attended a series of meetings. I was called to meet with the Speaker of the Knesset, Yuli Edelstein. I used the meeting as an opportunity to ask his advice regarding how he thought I could be the best possible MK. I worked hard throughout the 19th Knesset to heed his sage advice which included to attend and take part in as many debates and votes as possible and to stay away from a lot of the showmanship which MK's use to gain face time in the media.

The director general of the Knesset, Ronen Plaut, met with me to explain how he and his office could be of help during my time in office. The most daunting meeting was with the chief Knesset attorney, Eyal Yanon. He explained to me how life will never be the same and how every action of mine was subject to public scrutiny. During that meeting it began to hit me that, indeed, life was now different by virtue of becoming a public figure.

Each new member of Knesset is given the opportunity to deliver an inaugural address. We were told that this is the address which would always serve as the baseline for our accomplishments in the Knesset and would define us to other members and to the broad public. It would also be the very first opportunity to speak at the Knesset podium. I spent more time preparing for that speech than any I had ever given in my life, or any I have given since. I worked to craft a focused message that remained interesting from beginning to end, and, of course, I practiced the Hebrew. The last thing I wanted to do was to commit any serious Hebrew error while delivering such an important and high-profile speech.

Walking up to that podium the first time was quite scary. When I got up there, I didn't even allow myself to pause in order to look around the room. I was afraid of being overwhelmed by the experience. So, I walked right up and began speaking immediately. With the exception of a small, almost unnoticeable stumble on words at the very beginning, the speech flowed and I felt very connected to my message. The speech had emotional components to it – thanking my family and describing my late father whose example

16

helped me reach that podium. I played mental games to make sure I didn't cry, since I figured it would be a fiasco for a Knesset member to show that kind of weakness while giving an inaugural address. I maintained my composure despite the sadness I felt when talking about my father, suffering internally that he was not there with me to share the experience.

*Screenshot from the Knesset Channel during my inaugural address.*
*The caption reads: MK Dov Lipman, Yesh Atid: "The time has come to*
*restore the value of combining Torah study with going to work."*

Well, so much for my pretending to be so tough. A few days later, MK Yaakov Peri, the former head of the Israel Internal Security Agency (the "Shabak), a position in Israel which defines the person as "Mr. Tough," delivered his inaugural address and was very choked up as he spoke about this good friend, Amnon Lipkin-Shahak, who passed away earlier that year. On that day I learned that it is most certainly okay for an MK to show sincere human emotions at the Knesset podium.

As I was finishing the speech and stepping down from the podium, I saw my female colleagues in Yesh Atid holding flowers. After every inaugural speech, the other MK's traditionally come and congratulate the speakers with handshakes and hugs. The Yesh Atid party had gelled into a real, close family unit during and after the election campaign. There was genuine respect for one another. We had actual "get together" nights when we got to know one another better and to simply have a good time in each other's company. While, of course, if a woman sticks out her hand I will shake it, they chose to show their respect for me as an Orthodox Jew. All the males, starting with Yair Lapid who sat closest to the podium, gave me massive hugs, and each woman handed me a rose. I held onto those roses which, to me, symbolize our ability to respect one another and for the religious and secular populations to live in harmony and unity.

It was the perfect way for me to usher in what can be described as the official start of my Knesset career.

**Close connection with my colleagues in Yesh Atid
captured in these two pictures with deputy finance
minister MK Mickey Levy (top) and education
minister MK Rabbi Shai Piron (bottom)**

# COMMITTEES

MK Ofer Shelah, our faction chairman, asked me which committees I wanted to join. During our pre-Knesset classes, the speakers talked about how difficult it is to be effective in more than two committees. Therefore, I decided to ask for one committee in order to concentrate my energies on that committee. Since one of my main focuses in the Knesset was to assist English-speaking immigrants and the Ethiopian community along with improving Israel's relationship with Diaspora communities, I asked for the Immigration, Absorption and Diaspora Affairs Committee. The party accepted that request and also placed me in the Knesset House Committee which deals with procedural issues in the Knesset.

The chairman of the Immigration, Absorption, and Diaspora Affairs Committee, fellow Yesh Atid MK Yoel Razvozov, named me as his replacement to head the committee in his absence. He also told me that I can call a hearing about any issue I want. That is precisely what I did.

*Sitting in as chairman of the Immigration, Absorption*
*and Diaspora Affairs Committee*

I attended all committee hearings when they didn't conflict with crucial votes in the House Committee and focused my attention on specific issues: making the absorption process easier for English speaking immigrants including simplifying the process for new immigrants to obtain Israeli driver's licenses, Ethiopian Israelis with direct family members in Ethiopia being refused the right to immigrate, and the fight against anti-Semitism.

*Walking quickly between committees – a constant juggling act*

The hearing on the first issue was a difficult one, with Transportation Ministry officials making it quite clear that they didn't anticipate any changes in government policy. This was one of my first exposures to "veteran ministry officials." These are people who are not political appointees and who have been in their professional positions in ministries for years – oftentimes decades. They are not very open to any major changes, to put it lightly. We invited new immigrants to tell their nightmare stories regarding how difficult it was for them to obtain an Israeli license but this did not seem to sway these officials.

Thanks to the immense pressure that we put on the Transportation Ministry over a long period of time, we managed to force a minor change in policy. In the past, immigrants who failed their driving test twice had to then take a theory test. This created major struggles for those many new immigrants who fail their driver's test twice and simply cannot pass a theory test. Fortunately, the ministry agreed to drop the theory test requirement. I continue to be in touch with Transportation Ministry officials to try to find ways to ease the overall process on new immigrants.

Another issue which I brought to the committee was the difficulty for nurses to move to Israel. The Health Ministry had a policy which prevented nurses from taking their licensing exam until they actually arrived in Israel as new immigrants. This meant that they would have to go months without earning a living, something which most new immigrants cannot afford. As I began to learn more about this problem it became even more absurd as I discovered that there is a shortage of nurses in Israel. On the heels of a long and grueling process, we finally got to a meeting with the relevant authorities in the ministry. When I asked them why they insist on this policy I received a one word answer which I got used to hearing about other issues as well: "Kacha." This means "because this is the way it is." I responded that I will not accept "Kacha" when it is preventing new immigrants from coming and prolonging the shortage of nurses in Israel. We ultimately had the policy changed, hopefully opening the door to hundreds of nurses who want to make Israel their home.

The issue of the Ethiopian immigrants separated from their loved ones has been close to my heart ever since I visited their relatives in Gondar several years ago. It makes no sense that we brought people here, and their parents, siblings or children are not being permitted to join them. The committee hearing on the issue put pressure on the Interior Ministry and the minister agreed to form a committee for families to appeal the forced separation from their family members. I am sad that elections were called before we were able to complete the oversight of this process, but I am following the 20th Knesset's Immigration and Absorption Committee's oversight on this issue and will continue to be involved.

Fighting anti-Semitism was the most frustrating aspect of my experience in this committee. We were presented with scary statistics about the rise of anti-Semitism throughout the world and especially throughout Europe.

We met with the government in order to explore what strategies were being taken to combat anti-Semitism and BDS. I never once saw a clear government strategy to deal with this issue. Seeing this lack of strategy, I called and chaired a hearing involving the many wonderful organizations which fight anti-Semitism, especially on-line. Amazingly, they reported that this was the first time in years that they were called together, as a unit, for a session to discuss how they can best work together and how the government can assist them in their efforts. The feedback was clear. They need straightforward, unified messages from the government and must receive information in real time about any IDF actions which can otherwise be twisted and distorted to turn public opinion against Israel. A lack of quick communication from the army's spokesperson unit and a method to quickly disseminate the truth leads to our losing the public diplomacy war.

My colleague in Yesh Atid, Ronen Hoffman, worked on this issue for months and wrote legislation which creates a clear flow of information to ambassadors around the world and to the many organizations dealing with this issue, especially on social media. The law established a mechanism for the Israeli Defense Forces to share whatever information it can, in real time, regarding any events or episodes that occur or situations which arise which could be used by the BDS and anti-Israel community to claim IDF abuse and mistreatment of the Palestinians. Unfortunately, the law stalled due to a disagreement between the Prime Minister's Office and the Foreign Ministry over who would be in control of this infrastructure and stand at the top of this information pyramid. Our only chance to fight the well-organized and well-funded BDS movement is a clear strategy and significant investment to implement that strategy.

As a committee we investigated the issue of working with the on-line companies whose sites are used to spread the hate. We found that European countries were willing to crack down on European companies, but our greatest struggle was in dealing with companies like Facebook and YouTube which are based in the United States where free speech laws make it difficult to act against anti-Semitic sites and posts. We decided to work with members of Congress to make changes to these laws, to enable us to fight this battle. After recognizing the societal harm involved, the

U.S has made progress in overlooking free speech constraints in order to combat problems such as child pornography. The same must happen regarding anti-Semitism. Congress needs to pass legislation to enable us to work with these companies to close all anti-Semitic sites and reject all anti-Semitic posts. This is an effort which Yesh Atid will continue to pursue from the opposition.

Serving on the Knesset House Committee played a very important role in my learning more about how the Knesset functions on a procedural level and even more about the behind the scenes politicking involved in the passage of legislation and setting the Knesset agenda. Some of the greatest committee-related drama took place in the House Committee, as coalition parties threatened to torpedo legislation of other coalition parties if their laws and platforms were not advanced.

The most standard gimmick used to accomplish this related to assigning a committee to prepare legislation. The Knesset secretary assigns the appropriate committee for all laws. But the moment the law passes, any MK can call out that they want the law to go to a different committee. They don't need to explain why and the committee which they call out can be completely inappropriate for the law. (The MK's of United Torah Judaism would routinely call out "Committee of Science and Technology" - the committee chaired by their MK, Moshe Gafni, for any law which they disliked.) The moment an MK calls out a different committee, the issue must be brought before the House Committee for a vote. Parties threaten to vote in favor of sending the law to a committee whose chairman won't bring the law to a hearing or will stall the return of the law to the Knesset floor, effectively holding hostage the coalition parties who want the law to pass. This was actually the committee which played one of the strongest roles in the collapse of the 19th Knesset, as the committee chairman, MK Yariv Levin, refused, per the instructions of the prime minister, to bring certain Yesh Atid proposals to the committee for committee assignments.

The House Committee is also the place where decisions are made regarding debates in the plenum and visiting dignitaries. For example, before a debate about a controversial law – such as the law regarding the African refugees, or major issues of religion and state and, most certainly, for the state budget - the House Committee determines, in advance, how long the opposition will be given to speak against the law. This could be as many as 12 hours or more but there is always a limit placed so that the MK's know when to come for the vote. This arrangement is one of the reasons why viewers on Knesset TV are often perplexed by an empty room while MK's stand at the podium and criticize legislation. We knew there would not be a vote and after a few hours of discussion and debate we move on to other things – including going home to our families. There were a few times when the opposition and coalition could not come to an agreement regarding the time and method of the debate and we stayed at the Knesset until the early morning hours. I slept in my office twice on these occasions – one time awakened when a member of the Knesset cleaning service came in to clean my office.

The hearings regarding the visits of foreign dignitaries were generally uneventful. We voted on the schedules for the visits and also voted to allow foreign dignitaries to speak in their mother tongues from the Knesset podium since the only languages officially sanctioned in the Knesset are Hebrew and Arabic. The only controversy erupted when Martin Shultz, president of the European Union, asked to speak in his native German. MK Moshe Feiglin expressed his discontent for German to be spoken in the Jewish parliament. However, veteran MK's pointed out that the Knesset had already crossed that line with the visits of previous visitors who spoke German, including Chancellor Angela Merkel in 2008.

After we were in office for about a year MK Ofer Shelah asked me to serve on the Knesset Finance Committee. My appointment to that Committee took me by surprise. This "upgrade" in committee assignment meant a complete change in schedule and focus. Finance Minister Yair Lapid set up a procedure which empowered committee members to be prepared and on top of every government financial transfer which would go through our committee. Every Thursday we would receive an email detailing every single transfer – where the money was coming from and where it was ending up. We had the right to ask questions regarding any transfer which we viewed as problematic. The representatives to the Finance Ministry for the beneficiary ministry were required to answer our queries. This enabled us to vote only after we knew precisely where the funds were going and why.

I didn't realize how unique, efficient and honest this system was until Prime Minister Netanyahu fired Yair Lapid form his position as Finance Minister. Netanyahu took his place as acting Finance Minister. A few days later, I awoke at 6:00a.m. to find an e-mail informing me that there would be a Finance Committee hearing that day at 9:00a.m. The e-mail included a long list of more transfer funds than I had ever seen before for one meeting. There was no way we could read through all that material by 9:00a.m., but there we were three hours later, voting on the transfer of hundreds of millions of shekel with no information or explanations. To my great dismay, the Knesset did not do its job of overseeing the government that day and the people of Israel had their taxpayer money being transferred to all kinds of interests without their elected officials making sure it was being used properly. There were also numerous individuals I had never seen before in the committee room that day, walking around trying to convince MK's to vote for the transfers. It turns out that two of them were arrested as part of the Yisrael Beiteinu scandal. I was witness to corruption. On the one hand I was sad to see this, and did not vote in favor or against any transfers for which no explanations were given. On the other hand I was proud to know that my party had established a protocol to prevent this from happening, and that while we were in power this corruption did not occur.

One other negative episode during my time in the Finance Committee remains etched in my mind. There was heavy traffic on Highway 1 and all the committee members sent messages that we would be late for the 9:00a.m. meeting. I walked into the committee room at 9:07a.m., only to learn that committee chairman MK Nissim Slomiansky (Bayit Yehudi) had already voted on the transfer of hundreds of millions of shekel for education – by himself!! There was no other MK in the room. This was a transfer which I supported but I sided with the MK's who lashed out at the chairman for voting on such a transfer without the involvement of other MK's and without a proper debate and opportunity for opposition.

I believe a rule should be enacted requiring a quorum of MK's present in the Finance Committee in order to approve any financial transfers. This would provide citizens the most basic assurance that there is some degree of proper Knesset oversight regarding the way government funds are spent.

Serving on the Finance Committee was a whole new experience for me, both in terms of the world of finance and the Hebrew terminologies used in this committee. As my first step, I did a significant amount of homework about economics and the Finance Ministry. Then, every week I would read through the documents and, after looking up the translations of unfamiliar words, I would note the new ones and work on not just remembering them but incorporating them into my conversations both in the committee and in the Knesset, in general.

**Voting on a motion in the Finance Committee**

Aside from working at my three regular committee assignments, I also served as a non-voting member of the special committee which dealt with the issue of equality in national service for the ultra-Orthodox population. It was an honor to participate in what I view as one of the most important and necessary changes in Israel today – the integration of the ultra-Orthodox community into society and especially the Israel Defense Forces.

The fact that the ultra-Orthodox don't participate in military or national service creates significant polarization and I believe there is no reason for ultra-Orthodox young men not to serve in an official capacity. We created a system which enables those who truly study Torah day and night as their only pursuit to continue studying and in the legislation which we wrote and passed in this committee, we labeled their Torah study as their service to the people of Israel. We also established frameworks which allow all religious people to adhere to their religious principles and values while serving either in the army or in national service.

*Engaged in a debate with MK Yaakov Litzman (United Torah Judaism) about haredim serving in the IDF*

An interesting phenomenon occurred in the hearings of this committee. The ultra-Orthodox MK's would often talk strategy among themselves – right next to me. I am not sure if they thought I didn't understand the Hebrew or if they thought I was really focused on other things, but I actually gained important information from some of these situations – information which helped us understand what they were going to do to try to torpedo or change the legislation. This enabled me and my colleagues to be prepared and deal with the challenges which these MK's often presented.

**Ultra-Orthodox MK's Moshe Gafni, Meir Porush, and Ariel Attias planning their strategy right next to me in the committee for the legislation regarding the draft and the ultra-Orthodox**

I also attended many hearings of the education committee which dealt with the issue of preventing the suffering of animals and the law and justice committee which dealt with the issue of conversion reform. Balancing all of these assignments was not an easy task but there is no doubt that the committee hearings and the more private meetings which take place on the side during committee hearings is where the real parliamentary work took place.

Committee hearings, especially in the finance committee, were often quite long. Opposition members would often do their best to filibuster and make it difficult for us to vote on whatever issue was being debated. The ultra-Orthodox MK's would use this tactic on any issue which they saw as damaging to their community. One time this dragged on for ours so I used the time for – Torah study – the very value which they claimed to be fighting for. The pictures of me studying religious texts sitting alongside ultra-Orthodox MK's who sought to waste everyone's time with their filibuster spread like wildfire through the ultra-Orthodox media.

Among the hundreds of hearings which I experienced in all of these committees, I can never forget something unique that happened prior to one of them. I entered the Knesset Finance Committee room for what I knew would be hours of a grueling debate over the budget. Coalition and opposition members arrived, tired after hours of pre-hearing preparation, and on edge as a result of uncertainty regarding the direction the government. I saw a few MK's huddling, and was surprised to see that they included opposition and coalition MK's together. I assumed that a deal was being worked out to spare us all hours of debate. As I approached the MK's, I saw they were watching a video on an iPad, and many were declaring: "I can't believe it!" I joined them and saw what they were looking at: a replay of the incredible, acrobatic catch made by New York Giants wide receiver, Odell Beckham, Jr. The hearing began a few minutes later, a less raucous and contentious debate than usual which I believe was due to the unified excitement and enthusiasm over "the catch" which we all just watched together.

Serving on these committees, I learned pretty quickly that the Knesset committee system is not optimal. I recall when I interned in Congress - and as anyone can see on C-Span - how any person appearing before a Congressional hearing is sworn in. They actually swear to tell the truth. While, of course, that system is also not foolproof, the fact that someone can be prosecuted for lying before Congress automatically means that more people are telling the truth. I sat in Knesset committee hearings and listened to people speaking to us, usually with guests contradicting each other, without any mechanism to know who was telling the truth and who was committing perjury. There was no way to prevent them from lying if it suited their interests. I believe that the Knesset should introduce some form of oath before guests speak before an official committee.

**Raising questions about a procedural issue during a committee hearing**

In order for this change to occur, something else would have to change regarding the set up and format of these hearings. Most committee meetings were what is known as a "balagan," with no real order or schedule of speakers. Committee chairmen would simply switch off between MK's commenting and guests speaking their minds. There was never a feeling of specific people coming and truly reporting to the committee, with each MK asking their questions and the guest being required to answer them. As a result, sessions which could have been far more productive ended with little or no clarity and with lost opportunities to make progress on important issues. I have already begun the process of attempting to change these two elements of committee work in the Knesset to make these hearings more functional and productive.

# THE PLENUM

As the 19<sup>th</sup> Knesset came to an end, I was summoned to the office of the Knesset Speaker, MK Yuli Edelstein. He informed me that I was to be honored for voting in the plenum that term more than any other MK.

To be honest, I viewed showing up and voting on legislation as my job and my responsibility. I did not feel that I had done something special. However, the honor did reflect my love for being in the plenum, having the opportunity to participate in the fascinating debates and to be part of the process of the Knesset's most important task.

I will never forget the moment when we walked into the plenum for the first time and were shown our seats. All of us stood in place in awe – recognizing the special moments in history which had taken place in that beautiful room and internalizing that we were now about to take our own places in that hallowed chamber.

The first thing you learn about the plenum is that there are rules regarding who can go where and when. The only people permitted on the actual Knesset floor are MK's and the ushers. Staff members with access to the room are not allowed to cross an invisible line, the top of the two steps leading onto the actual floor. MK's may not sit in the seats at the government table in the middle of the room. If you want to talk to a minister you either have to stand next to their seat, or they will go with you to vacant seats in other places in the room. No eating or drinking is permitted in the plenum. There is an area behind the main room where they serve coffee and, when the plenum runs late, they serve cookies, pastries, and vegetables. It is also against the rules to speak on a telephone in the plenum. Many MK's found creative ways to circumvent this. Occasionally, there were some MK's who boldly spoke on the phone until they were escorted out by an usher.

*The view from right behind my seat - a non-electronic vote by hand on the state budget*

The plenum is in session on Mondays, Tuesdays, and Wednesdays. Mondays and Tuesdays begin at 4:00p.m. and Wednesdays at 11:00a.m. Mondays begin with no-confidence motions against the government followed by actual no-confidence votes. These are followed by votes on government laws. Tuesdays begin with "one-minute speeches," followed by votes on laws in which there is consensus between the coalition and opposition, followed by points of order and discussions on those points. Wednesdays begin with MK questions to government ministers ("Sheiltot") followed by votes on private member laws, followed by additional points of order and discussions on those points.

The no-confidence votes on Monday are the most exciting time of the week in the plenum, not because of any drama since the outcome is known in advance, but because everyone is there. This is the time for MK's to catch up with ministers and for ministers to grab MK's if they need them for something. I would come to the plenum with a list of ministers I had to talk to about certain issues and there was a constant "game" of trying to grab them before anyone else did when they became available. Without a doubt, this was among the most productive hours of the week. The votes, themselves, are anti-climactic because the coalition whips always make sure that everyone is there in order to vote to preserve the government. But there is an incredible energy in the room as the vote nears and the plenum begins to fill.

The controversy surrounding government legislation often led to hours of debate and very late Monday nights. I slept in my office twice – leaving the plenum at around 3:30a.m. and at 5:00a.m. following those long nights. One debate related to a law requiring a minimum number of women on the committee that chooses the religious judges. The ultra-Orthodox parties filibustered but ultimately yielded for a vote at 3:30a.m. The second time related to a series of three pieces of legislation: the drafting of the ultra-Orthodox, raising the electoral threshold and requiring a national referendum vote before giving up any Israeli land in an agreement with the Palestinians. All of these touch on a wide range of sensitivities. In the end, the opposition actually stayed away from the plenum during the voting on these laws, but one night of debate with the possibility of a vote being called at any moment kept us in the plenum until 5:00a.m.

Not all Knesset members stayed up that late and, in general, the plenum was only full at around 6:00p.m. on Mondays when we voted on opposition no-confidence measures or for special events. How are MK's able to be absent? The answer is a Hebrew word, "kizuz." If an MK does not want to stay for a plenum, he or she can find someone from the opposite side of the room to offset them, and then both leave – one member of the coalition together with one from the opposition. There were MK's from both sides who did this regularly and were rarely seen in the plenum sessions. I strongly believe that this is an abrogation of our responsibility as elected officials and never made use of this arrangement except when I was called away for Knesset business or personal emergencies which, thank God, were rare.

The "one minute speeches" which begin every Tuesday sessions present an opportunity for MK's to speak about any topic they choose. My colleague, MK Boaz Toporovsky, used the one-minute speech every week to read the names of people who were killed in traffic accidents that week to help raise awareness about the issue of traffic safety. For me, it was a great way to work my way into feeling more comfortable speaking in the plenum, and I tried to find a meaningful message to share on a weekly basis. This could be based on something that was happening in current events, talking about an organization or institution which I visited that week or simply using it as a platform to share an idea of mine. For most of the 19th Knesset I read my one-minute speeches but towards the end of the term I felt comfortable enough with the language and the timing to speak without reading from a written text.

*Delivering a one-minute speech – reading from a prepared text, and*
*then the comfort to simply speak - as seen on the Knesset Channel*

My biggest fear, especially in a speech where there was a time constraint and I felt somewhat rushed, was that I would make a major mistake in Hebrew. Thank God, I only pronounced one word wrong and the mistake wasn't bad enough to become a focus of jokes in the Knesset or the press. I was praising the appointment of a haredi woman to serve as a dean at Bar Ilan University and instead of "dikanit," the word for "dean," I said "daikanit," which means "precise" – not a terrible mistake, and it went unnoticed.

The most surprising moment in these one-minute speeches was when MK Yaakov Asher of United Torah Judaism verbally attacked me by name. Standing just a few feet away from me in the plenum, he used his one-minute speech to attack comments that I made earlier in the day against MK Moshe Gafni from his party. Gafni had said that when he sees women wearing tefilin (phylacteries) at the Western Wall, it "breaks his heart." I replied that "I don't understand what MK Gafni is doing looking at the women's side of the Western Wall," and then explained that while, in my family, the women do not wear these ritual objects, I don't understand why we are trying to stop women who want to wear them from doing so. MK Asher said that his "blood was boiling" over this encounter. He then turned to me and said, "I ask one thing from MK Lipman. Don't speak as a 'haredi' (ultra-Orthodox) when you're not really one. Don't make a fool out of people when you entered Knesset just because someone made a mistake and thought that because of how you look, you're haredi."

I turned to the Speaker of the Knesset to see if I could respond, and he signaled for me to come up towards the front of the room where the Knesset secretary informed me that there is a clause in the Knesset by-laws which gives an MK the right to respond if another MK attacks him or her by name.

I had to submit a quick, handwritten note to the Speaker, quoting that specific clause, and then I was given the right to speak from the main Knesset podium, as opposed to the one-minute speeches which are delivered from the side microphones. This gave me the opportunity to give a firm, harsh response. I stood at the podium and said, among other things, that God is the One who judges people's level of religious observance and not MK Asher. I also explained that someone who observes the Bible does not speak the way MK Asher just spoke.

In general, the one-minute speeches were a good time to hear what was on the minds of other MK's and to be part of the lively discussions which often ensued when an MK touched on a hot-button topic. The remainder of Tuesdays was for legislation in which there was consensus. I always remained for those votes. These were followed by points-of-order sessions which I attended if I was speaking or if the topic was of interest to me.

These points of order are the times when an MK must learn the art of speaking to an empty room. There are situations when, aside from the sitting Speaker, there will be one minister in the room (as mandated in the Knesset by-laws) and just one or two other MK's. However, knowing that there are tens of thousands watching on the Knesset channel, I always spoke and looked around the room as if it were full.

The plenum begins at 11:00a.m. on Wednesdays and starts off with "sheiltot" – MK questions for ministers. The questions have to be approved by the Knesset presidium (the Speaker and his deputies), and ministers are given several days to prepare their answers. MK's may ask follow-up questions, as well. Frankly, these question sessions are more of an opportunity for publicity than anything else. It gives any MK the chance to make some waves by asking a minister a tough question, and the ministers certainly use their answer time as a platform to get a message out - either about the question that was asked or anything else they may have on their minds. Real work in changing things via ministers occurs behind the scenes – usually with the MK's staff members working closely with the minister's staffers.

Around an hour into the Wednesday plenum, we shift to private-member legislation. This generally begins with laws which the government has decided to accept. The MK presents the law before the plenum and opposition members can then voice their objections if they signed up to speak. Those votes generally went pretty smoothly. Then the fun would begin as laws from opposition MK's that had been rejected by the coalition were brought to the floor. The sponsoring MK is given ten minutes to try to convince coalition members to break from coalition discipline and support their law. A government minister then responds and explains why the law has been rejected by the government. The vote then takes place, and the law is defeated. (This was the reality during the 19th Knesset with a government of 68 mandates - the opposition never presented a real threat in winning a vote. This changed in the 20th Knesset, with a coalition consisting of the minimum 61 mandates and the opposition having 59. The opposition succeeded in passing the initial reading of a Yesh Atid law which the government rejected.) Those Wednesdays are very long and the plenum is in session during lunch hours. MK's typically go across the hallway to eat lunch in the MK and minister cafeteria (more on this later) and the party whips can be seen running through the cafeteria urging MK's to hurry into the plenum to make sure they vote against these laws. Bells are sounded throughout the Knesset building to indicate that a vote will be taking place shortly and, once the vote is officially called, there are ten seconds to vote. The scene of MK's running through the halls and rushing to their seats to vote, including numerous collisions in the plenum as this panic transpired, was quite entertaining.

There are times when the coalition MK's actually pay attention as the opposition MK's present a law – something which I tried to do whenever possible – and are convinced that the government has made a mistake and the coalition should re-explore supporting the law. When this happens, there is an incredible buzz and quite a bit of pandemonium in the room as coalition MK's lobby the coalition leadership not to topple the law. The option available is for the opposition MK to shift the legislation from a law to a point of order. As a point of order, it would then be sent to committee and a process begins to amend the law to enable the coalition to support it. Once those changes are made, the law would then return to the ministerial committee for legislation and on to the Knesset for passage.

*Listening attentively to an MK presenting legislation prior to a vote*

I was once part of the shifting of one important piece of opposition legislation to a point of order. An MK from Shas proposed legislation that the package people received from internet companies should be automatically filtered, thus blocking pornographic material. Those consumers who wanted that content in their package would need to request it. I believed that this was the right move for a Jewish state which should be built on core Jewish values, and basic morality and decency should be a part of that. (I had actually considered initiating similar legislation myself.) A number of us in the plenum rallied the coalition chairman, MK Yariv Levin, to accept the law as a point of order and not allow it to come to a vote whereby the coalition would reject it as the coalition leadership had initially decided.

Coalition members may not vote against any law accepted by the coalition through a majority vote in the ministerial committee for legislation. If they feel that they cannot vote in favor of a certain law, they may abstain, usually by absenting themselves from the room during the vote. Coalition members who vote against the coalition are subject to consequences, including losing committee assignments and being stripped of the ability to pass their own legislation.

I abstained from voting on coalition legislation a few times. The most glaring of these was a law which was initiated by MK Moshe Mizrachi of the Labor party which I proudly co-sponsored. The law said that an MK or minister who was found guilty of crimes of moral turpitude could never return to public office. The law was rejected, largely because of Avigdor Liberman's Yisrael Beiteinu party, and instead, the coalition accepted a law which increased their ban on public service from seven to 14 years after time served. This meant that coalition members had to vote against the permanent ban. I could not do so. I made sure not to be in the room for the vote while determining that my vote would not make the crucial difference between the law's passage or not. (I am proud that my Yesh Atid party has resubmitted MK Mizrachi's law in the 20th Knesset and am not proud that the coalition rejected it.)

*Saying "good night" to Finance Minister Yair Lapid and MK*
*Penina Tamanu-Shata after a long night of voting*

Wednesdays ended with additional points of order which could last for hours, sometimes until 7:00 or 8:00 in the evening.

The plenum is also where the most special events occur. I was privileged to be part of an incredible day in the Knesset: voting for the president of Israel. The president is elected by the 120 members of Knesset, so for months the candidates held private meetings with us and made their case for why they would be the best president (some candidates asked for multiple meetings and some actually begged me for my vote!) On that special day, the entire Knesset gathered in the plenum with the candidates seated around the room – MK's in their assigned seats and non-MK's in designated seats bordering the plenum floor. MK's were then called up by name and given an envelope by the Knesset secretary. The MK then entered a special Knesset plenum voting booth to cast a ballot. The drama was intense. Since no candidate won a majority, we went to a second round of voting and the same process was repeated. In this case, the two remaining candidates, Reuven Rivlin and Meir Sheetrit, sitting MK's, were sitting just two rows apart from each other – right near my seat. There was intense lobbying going on leading up to the vote, with pressure being put on all of us from all different directions. To lighten the mood, many of us took selfies with the two candidates. I got one with both of them together.

I was happy once the elections were over because I felt that the tension in the building was distracting us from our parliamentary work. But it was a true honor to take part in that process.

There were special visits from dignitaries during the 19th Knesset. The speeches delivered by UK Prime Minister Cameron, French President Hollande, EU President Schmidt, and Canadian Prime Minister Harper were the highlights. There was always a fear of MK's interrupting these dignitaries – with the right wing possibly attacking someone who sounded too left, and the left, or more specifically the Arabs, attacking someone who sounded too right. And both did occur. However, despite those interruptions, I found that these visits brought tremendous honor to the Knesset and that these leaders walked away from their visits with positive impressions of the Knesset and Israel. The funeral for former Prime Minister Ariel Sharon brought United States Vice-President Joseph Biden to the Knesset and his speech, delivered outside the building, was one of the most uplifting and inspiring that I heard at the Knesset.

The long hours in the plenum require MK's to find ways to pass the time. The prime minister, for example, brings books to read during long debates, voting on the budget and specific legislation. His books were generally in English and, for a considerable amount of time, he was reading about Churchill. My colleague, Ruth Calderon, spent the time very openly studying religious texts – the Mishna and the Talmud. Some of the greatest moments came when members of the Shas party would join her in study or in discussion about a controversial topic in the texts. I would spend some of the time studying religious texts using my iPad instead of opening actual books. I also used this time to answer constituents' e-mails and Facebook posts.

**MK Ruth Calderon studying Talmud right in front of me. To the left you can see the Prime Minister reading a book.**

The plenum is a place for show. The ministers and MK's know that the cameras are rolling and a simple decision to sit down and talk to a specific MK could lead to excellent pictures and immense speculation among political commentators regarding the possible contents of the conversation. Dramatic speeches from the Knesset podium are also for show and are often used to play to the cameras.

The room where the real work takes place is behind the plenum, not under the scrutiny of the cameras or any reporters. That room with many couches, is where they serve hot drinks throughout the day and food (pastries and vegetables) when the sessions run late. This is where two MK's who were screaming at each other in the plenum just moments before can be found on the couches either talking about personal, family related topics or actual work and professional cooperation. I wish the broader public could see the dynamics in this hidden room. Since all they see is the public show, they assume that there is no cooperation. This engenders animosity between populations along political and, sometimes, religious lines. If they would see the cooperation and the extent of respect and even friendship that exists across party and ideological lines it would do a great deal to calm those tensions.

**MK Meshulam Nahari, member of the Shas party discussing a section of Talmud with MK Ruth Calderon - an example of cross party camaraderie**

One example which I will never forget came during the height of the debate regarding the draft of the ultra-Orthodox community. Tempers were running high and the passionate debates reached a climax. Suddenly there was a pause in the action due to some technical procedural issues that arose and one of the religious MK's called out "Maariv," indicating that they wanted to gather together to pray the evening services. MK's from almost all of the parties put aside the ideological debate and joined together to pray in that back room. When we finished, it was back to the plenum where the arguing resumed.

My strongest and most meaningful moment from the plenum came in late June 2014. We were in session when official word came that the three kidnapped boys' were found dead. The Speaker walked in, made the announcement, and called off the remainder of the session. We quietly left that hallowed chamber to join the rest of the country in mourning.

# LEGISLATION

The primary task of a parliament is to initiate and pass legislation. Knesset members are expected to write and pass new laws that will improve the lives of our constituents.

The process of a bill becoming a law sounded relatively uncomplicated when it was explained during our pre-Knesset orientation. I quickly learned, however, how in actuality it is quite complex. The first step is to write the law. Most MK's need outside help from an attorney experienced in writing laws in order to get through this first step. Once the law is written, an MK tries to enlist others – preferably MK's representing the widest range of parties possible – to co-sponsor the law.

*Signing my first law soon after entering office*

The broader the support base, the better chance the law has to pass. Once the law has additional signatures, it is submitted to the Knesset secretary who sends the law to the Knesset's legal department. There, attorneys study the law to determine whether it is a reiteration of pre-existing laws or if there are any controversies which from the outset would rule out passage of the law. Once the attorneys approve the law, the law receives a "pei," an official number, and it is "placed on the Knesset table." The law must sit there for a minimum of 45 days before it can move on to the next step.

Once the 45 days are completed, the law CAN be brought to the ministerial committee for legislation. I say "can," because there are many factors which determine whether the law can make it to the committee. The first is the chair of the committee, the Justice Minister. The first lesson one learns about successfully passing legislation in the Knesset is the importance of establishing a relationship with the minister who chairs that committee and that minister's staff. When the new 33rd government was formed, the Justice Minister turned out to be Tzipi Livni, a person with whom I had no prior association. I quickly studied her interests and discovered that I could establish a rapport with her based on our mutual interest in preventing the unnecessary suffering of animals. I succeeded in doing this.

The second factor in a law making it to the ministerial committee is the numerical limitation on how many laws a party can present to the committee. An MK needs to work with the party leadership within the Knesset including the faction head, the faction administrator, the faction whip, and the faction secretary to make sure that the law makes it to that committee. More than once, miscommunications or misunderstandings between myself and any one of those administrators led to laws of mine not making it to that committee at the right time.

Once the law is on the docket for that crucial Sunday meeting of the ministerial committee for legislation, the real lobbying begins. The law requires a simple majority to pass and move to the Knesset floor – this means the sponsoring MK must reach out to a majority of the ministers in the committee in order to secure their support for the law. MK's must sit with the ministers from their own party to teach them the law and prepare them to argue on its behalf before the committee in order to win the majority victory. However, attaining a simple majority is not enough. Any one minister can "appeal" the law – an act which stops the law from proceeding to the Knesset for a vote. That appeal can send the law back to the committee, which means that it would have to be brought back for another vote on a different week, at the discretion of the committee chairman; or it can be appealed to the government. An appeal to the government - an extreme step - essentially buries the legislation, since the prime minister would need to decide to bring the law to a government vote despite the protest of one of his ministers – an act which could place the coalition in jeopardy. This is the reason, incidentally, why Yesh Atid and Bayit Yehudi joined together to keep the ultra-Orthodox parties out of the government. It wasn't due to any kind of personal or communal hatred, as was commonly expressed. Rather, it was a practical step because any one ultra-Orthodox minister would have had the power to stall any proposed legislation regarding religion and state, or changes in their community.

So the lobbying process must include securing the support of the justice minister, who must agree to bring the law to a vote to start the process, and who can also determine whether there will be a revote to override an appeal. It also requires fact finding and lobbying to make sure there is no minister who will fight the law at all costs, regardless of whatever politicking and give and take is undertaken to stop an appeal. If such a minister exists, the law has almost no chance of passing.

If the law passes the ministerial committee for legislation on Sunday, it comes to the Knesset floor that Wednesday for an initial reading ("kriya tromit"). The sponsoring MK is given either one minute from a side microphone or ten minutes from the Knesset podium to present the law (each party is allotted a certain amount of time to speak from the podium and the rest must be from the side microphones). MK's are given the opportunity to speak out against the law from the podium, and then the law is brought to a vote.

Once a law passes its initial reading, it is sent to committee. The Knesset presidium, made up of the Speaker and the deputy Speakers, determine to which committee the law is sent. If any MK yells out another committee while the Speaker announces the assigned committee, the law must go to the Knesset House Committee to make a final determination regarding the appropriate committee. A typical opposition tactic is to scream out other committees simply to delay the legislative process, since this requires the additional step of the House Committee convening, debating and voting.

Simply getting your vote to the committee hearing depends largely on the chairman of the committee. Therefore, an MK who wants to pass legislation must develop positive working relationships with the committee chairmen. Once the law makes it to the committee, the process can be long and drawn out with MK's, usually from the opposition, proposing addendums and adjustments and the law's budgetary impact scrutinized to the most minute detail. Once the law is voted on and passes in the committee, it comes back to the plenum for a first reading ("Kriya Rishona"), in which the sponsoring MK presents the law. A discussion ensues in which MK's may give their opinion about the law, and then it is voted on again. The law then returns to the committee, which prepares it for its second and third reading. Once it passes again in the committee, it returns to the Knesset where the committee chairman presents the law to the plenary.

During the committee process, parties submit their suggested adjustments to the law and the committee must vote for or against those suggested changes. Even after the committee rejects them, those suggested changes can be submitted as official reservations and then the Knesset must vote on those reservations before voting on the law. Once the law passes its second reading, it immediately goes to a third reading, and if it passes, it enters into the official law books.

We were told not to expect to successfully pass many laws and that for an MK to move two laws through to a third reading in one term is a massive success.

My own history in the 19ᵗʰ Knesset is a fascinating study of the challenges and obstacles an MK faces in the legislative process. I was not successful in bringing any laws to a final reading, but am happy that the laws I proposed led to substantive debate and discussion about the various issues and that colleagues in the 20ᵗʰ Knesset are continuing to push some of these laws through the process.

The Yesh atid party gave me the Knesset portfolios for the environment, public health, and preventing the suffering of animals. Even prior to the inauguration I began working on legislation in these realms. The first law which I placed on the Knesset table was to outlaw the importing of foie gras. Foie gras is fattened goose liver in which a tube is shoved down the throat of the goose, and it is then force-fed over and over to the point that it can barely stand and breathe on its own. It is a horrific process which is not only inhumane but also clearly violates the religious value of preventing the suffering of animals. Israel has already banned the production of this "delicacy" in Israel, a strong statement about our adherence to this value. After discussing the issue with my staff and learning more about the torture these animals experience, I decided to try to take our country to the next step in a unified effort to make a strong statement about our unwillingness to have this product in our country. A quick analysis of the various interests which might oppose the regulation convinced me that the law should pass smoothly. I spoke to a majority of ministers in the ministerial committee for legislation, and had a clear majority for the law to pass and move to the Knesset for a vote. The law passed the committee but the Yisrael Beiteinu party "appealed" the law – essentially stopping any possibility of moving it forward.

I spent significant time discussing the law with Agriculture Minister Yair Shamir from the Yisrael Beiteinu party, and ultimately came to a compromise with him. His primary concern was the banning of imports of any product, because this precedent could result in other countries banning the import of Israeli products. A country like ours, which is always under threat of boycotts, cannot risk such a step. I accepted this argument and agreed to have the terminology changed in committee to ban doing business with foie gras in Israel but that the word "import" would not appear in the law. This compromise enabled the law to come to the Knesset floor.

The law passed the committee and came to the Knesset floor one Wednesday afternoon. I gave a passionate speech about why the Knesset should pass the law and said: "I am proud to be a member in a Knesset that chose to place values before interests and fleeting pleasures. As public officials we have many responsibilities, one of them being to care for the rights of animals that depend entirely on us and can't care for themselves. I believe that this law will contribute not only to animals but also to Israel's global image. The time has come to get this soul-corrupting food out of Israel."

I noticed that throughout my close to ten-minute presentation, the ultra-Orthodox MK's were running around talking to each other and also on their phones. Sure enough, the vote passed 59-10 with all 10 ultra-Orthodox MK's in the room voting against the law. This perplexed me since Rabbi Ovadiah Yosef, spiritual leader of the ultra-Orthodox Shas party, wrote that the production of foie gras violated the Biblical command not to cause suffering to animals. They explained that they were afraid that a law of this kind, where Israel takes a strong stand against animal suffering, could be used against Jews around the world, and could lead to the outlawing of ritual slaughter. Their analysis was completely wrong as European Jewish groups wrote to me that this law would help their cause in the battle against such bans - demonstrating that we take animal suffering seriously strengthens the argument that our tradition of ritual slaughter does not violate this value and does not cause animals any such suffering.

I began the process of preparing the law for the committee when Finance Minister Yair Lapid asked to meet with me. He had just returned from a visit to Hungary, where he lobbied ministers and the parliament to fight against anti-Semitism. He sat down for his meeting with the Hungarian foreign minister about that important topic and the minister asked Yair if he could raise an unrelated topic before they discuss anti-Semitism. "We need to discuss and MK in your party, Lipman," he told Lapid. "You need to ask him to pull back on his law to ban foie gras in Israel. This is a major export of ours and could ultimately lead to economic damage to our country."

As Yair, who supported the law said to me: "I had to choose between fighting anti-Semitism and the foie gras law. You have to pull back and not move the law forward at this time." I, of course, agreed with him but remained stunned by this unexpected development. It was an instant lesson on how one never knows what interest or body can jump in and torpedo legislation.

A second piece of legislation which took unusual and unexpected turns related to agunot - women whose husbands refuse to the give them a divorce document, called a "get." Women in this situation are not permitted to remarry according to Jewish law and are essentially stuck, separated from their husbands with whom they no longer want to be married, yet at the same time, unable to move on and rebuild their lives.

I met to discuss the issue with the chief rabbi of Israel, Rabbi David Lau, and he suggested legislation to confront the worst violators - men who are actually in jail because of their refusal to give their wives a divorce. The Israeli penal system currently allows religious inmates to serve their time in the religious wing of the jails. The law which we wrote had two components: the first addressed the section of jail where the prison terms were being served. These men wake up every morning, attend prayer services, eat breakfast, and then spend their day learning in a comfortable study hall filled with religious books and texts. There is absolutely no pressure on them to give their wives a divorce. The proposed law stated that anyone serving in jail over their refusal to give a divorce cannot claim to be religious since they are not adhering to Jewish law. Thus, they no longer qualify to remain in the religious wing of the jail.

The second component related to their diet. All convicts incarcerated in Israel receive kosher food. Current Israeli law permits convicts who request it to receive "mehadrin" food, which are extra stringencies in kosher dietary laws taken into account in the preparation of food. Our new law stated that men who refuse to give their wives a divorce cannot claim to be so religious that they need this higher standard of kosher supervision and they must eat the regular kosher food. The chief rabbi believed that these men are so concerned about their status that this second component could actually compel a few of them to give their wives a divorce immediately following the bill's passage.

I did not foresee any reason this law could not move quickly through the Knesset, become law, and become the catalyst for these men to give their wives a divorce, thus enabling these women to move on with their lives and remarry. I assumed that the secular side would certainly encourage these measures and the religious side would certainly support a law which reflected the approval of the chief rabbi.

I was correct about the latter but not the former.

The secular side of the Knesset did take issue with the law. The first challenge came from the Knesset attorney's office. He called me into a meeting and questioned how we can create a scenario in which a murderer can claim to be religious and reside in the religious wing of jail, but a man who refuses to give his wife a divorce cannot. I replied that the issue at hand is not the severity of the crime. Rather, we must look at it this way: A person who murders could, in theory, regret his action immediately after the crime was committed and could sincerely claim that he is religious. But a man who refuses to give his wife a divorce - despite Jewish law mandating that he must do so - is continuing to transgress this command and Israeli law every single moment, and therefore, he cannot claim to be someone who adheres to religious commandments. It took significant time and effort, but ultimately I succeeded in convincing the Knesset attorney on this point. The law moved on to sit on the Knesset table and then to the ministerial committee for legislation.

Since this law included an element of time pressure because we want these men to give their wives a divorce as soon as possible, I asked MK Yariv Levin, chairman of the Knesset House Committee, to convene the committee which had the power to bypass the 45-day requirement for a law to move on. He agreed, and the law moved quickly to the ministerial committee for legislation. I began speaking to the ministers in my party to obtain what I assumed would be enthusiastic support for the law, before going to ministers from other parties. I quickly learned that there was another obstacle in the way. Secular ministers had a very difficult time with the clause that prohibits these men from eating the "mehadrin" food. They felt that this was a violation of basic human rights and we cannot prohibit any inmate from eating the food which they require according to their customs and traditions. I explained over and over that the regular kosher food is completely fine for these inmates to eat based on their religious beliefs and that there is no issue of human rights involved in denying them "mehadrin" food. But, it was to no avail, and in order for the law to pass the ministerial committee for legislation I had to commit to removing the clause about the food from the law.

The law then passed the ministerial committee and made its way to the Knesset floor, where it passed its initial reading. I immediately went to the chairman of the Knesset Justice Committee, the late MK Dudu Rotem, to ask him to bring the law to his committee as soon as possible. MK Rotem quickly spoiled my optimistic and enthusiastic mood when he told me that he does not think this law is so simple because of the overlapping of religious and secular courts, and it will be very complicated to place it onto the docket for this committee and have it pass through his committee. This was a new obstacle which was completely unforeseen, and stalled the progress of the legislation. The 19th Knesset disbanded soon after and my colleague, MK Aliza Lavie, resubmitted the law at the very start of the 20th Knesset.

I sponsored two other pieces of legislation related to the issue of agunot. The first dictated that if a husband has not given his wife a divorce 45 days after a Jewish court rules that he must do so, then we, as a state, step in and invalidate his passport, close his bank accounts, revoke his driver's license and make it illegal for any employer to hire him. I saw this action as being in complete consonance with the approach of Jewish communities throughout our history in dealing with such men - using communal pressure to "force" the husband to give his wife a divorce. Unfortunately, the Jewish Home party, which controlled the Religious Services Ministry, told me that they would stop the legislation from coming to a vote. They claimed that the rabbinate is the only body that can take such coercive measures against the husband and that my law weakened the rabbinate's power. Knowing that there was no chance for the law to even make it to a vote, I, with great sadness, did not even begin the legislative process for this bill.

The second law was aimed at preventing the problem of agunot in the future. The idea was to make prenuptial agreements a part of the official rabbinate process for weddings. According to Jewish law, this cannot be forced on the couple but it would be presented to them as a choice with the opportunity for them to refuse this option. A few other MK's sponsored similar laws and Justice Minister Tzipi Livni established a committee to study the issue and then turn it into a government law. This was a classic example of "establishing a committee" translating into "nothing will happen with it." The law got lost in that committee and did not move forward before the Knesset disbanded.

A law that I sponsored for public health, never moved forward because of a simple mistake. The law dictates that restaurants with a significant number of branches must list the calorie count on their set menus. This law exists throughout North American and Europe, and leads to public awareness and improved public health. I did all of the legwork necessary for this law to pass including obtaining the support of MK Avishai Braverman, chairman of the Economics Committee, where this law would have to pass as it goes through the Knesset. He actually co-signed the law after I agreed that, in committee, we would study the proper number of restaurant branches to which the law would apply in order to ensure that we don't hurt small businesses.

The ministers were lined up and the law was set to pass. On the day that the law came to the ministerial committee, chairwoman and Justice Minister Tzipi Livni sped through a list of laws which the committee was rejecting, and somehow this law was mistakenly placed on that list and rejected without any debate or discussion. When we heard that this happened, my staff made immediate contact with the staff of Health Minister Yael German, a member of the committee, and she immediately submitted an appeal. But Minister Livni had a policy to place appeals at the bottom of the docket of laws which come to the committee and the law did not make it back to the committee before the 19th Knesset was disbanded.

Three other laws that I sponsored were taken as government laws. This means that when a minister likes the legislation, he or she will often ask to take it as a government law under their own name. This gives more weight to the law and essentially assures the law's speedy approval. It also bypasses the need for an initial reading of the law and it can go straight to its first reading. The first such law was a law that the next election for chief rabbi will be for one chief rabbi instead of two. There is absolutely no reason for there to be both a Sephardic and Ashkenazic chief rabbi in a culture where families are blended and represent both cultures and in which all rabbis know the laws and customs of the other. Having a separate chief rabbi for each group creates polarization from the top since it dictates, as part of the religious establishment, that Sephardim and Ashkenazim are two distinct and separate groups. Minister of Religion Naftali Bennet took the proposed bill as a government law and moved it forward through the process.

The second law of mine which was taken as a government law was legislation requiring supermarkets to charge for the use of plastic bags. This is a policy which has transformed counties in the United States (including my hometown, Montgomery Country, Maryland) in creating an environmentally friendly society. Environmental Minister Amir Peretz asked me to allow him to make it his law on a governmental level and, of course, I agreed. The law passed its first reading and was then stalled in the Interior Committee chaired by MK Miri Regev because the Likud - as a result of quite a bit of urging from the ultra-Orthodox parties and lobbying from the companies that manufacture plastic bags - decided that it was actually against passing this legislation.

The third law which became a government law related to families like mine which foster puppies before they are trained to serve as guide dogs. Families are needed to keep the puppies for a year until they are old enough to be trained professionally. Until that time, the families train the dogs to be comfortable in public settings – a critical trait for a guide dog. Israeli law allows blind people to go anywhere with their dogs, and owners of malls, restaurants, etc. may not tell them to leave the dog outside. There was no law giving that same right to foster families of these puppies, and the refusal to allow them into public areas hinders their ability to become comfortable in public places. The unfortunate result is that this leads to dogs to fail the test as guide dogs.

*Bringing our puppy, Mando, who was trained to be a guide dog, to the Knesset with me*

My law said that anyone training a future guide dog has the same rights as a blind person with a guide dog and must be admitted to all public places with the dog. Welfare Minister Meir Cohen took the law as a government law but the government collapsed right after all the finishing touches were put on the law and it was ready to speed through the Knesset voting. I am so happy that the new Welfare Minister, Haim Katz, continued where we left off with this law and that the law is now making its way through the Knesset and will, hopefully, be signed into law.

There are other laws which I put into the legislative pipeline. One addressed the tens of thousands of healthy dogs that are put to death in Israel annually by pounds due to lack of space and the shortage of owners for these animals. The law outlawed killing healthy dogs alongside a second law with measures to control the pet population. Another law put much stricter rules in places regarding the use of trans-fat in Israeli products. Both of these laws never made it to the docket for the ministerial committee for legislation because our party had already filled its quota of laws from other MK's.

The frustrations I experienced during the legislative process taught me to understand why Knesset tradition says that any MK who enters two laws into the law books over the course of a four-year term is a successful legislator. While I am unhappy having none of my own, private member laws pass during the two years that we were in office, I proudly co-sponsored numerous laws that did pass and I am proud that even the laws that did not pass raised discussion and debate about the important issues which I tried to address.

# TASKFORCES

The moment the inauguration ceremony ended, the race to head Knesset "Shdulot" began. A "shdula" is a "taskforce" or "lobby," and heading a taskforce on a specific issue gives a Knesset member an important tool to impact these areas. Many MK's told me that this was a part of Knesset activity in which freshman members can drive change and make significant improvements in Israeli society. Therefore, I set out to establish a serious agenda via "shdulot."

My first step was to establish a Knesset taskforce to help the ultra-Orthodox ("Hareidi") population enter the workforce. Unemployment in this community, especially among males, is extremely high – above 50 percent. Since my initial decision to enter politics was largely related to my desire to see positive changes in the ultra-Orthodox community and to see it become part of the fabric of Israeli society instead of remaining isolated, this made the most sense as a first step. My staff and I worked quickly to arrange an opening event to enable us to field ideas and suggestions from experts on this issue. All agreed that helping this community get to work was the best thing we could do for them both in terms of raising them out of poverty and to help them become part Israeli society. The consensus was that the ultra-Orthodox community would not see this effort in a negative light or as an attempt to change their culture or traditions – a fear they generally have when outside forces try to bring initiatives to the community. I miscalculated.

This taskforce helped over 1,500 ultra-Orthodox people find jobs during our year and eight months in office. Two of our flagship projects had the greatest impact. The first was a partnership with "All Jobs," Israel's largest on-line employment agency and one of the top web sites used in Israel. Our taskforce worked with All Jobs to open a special division called

"All Jobs for Chareidim," in which companies would advertise positions for which they specifically wanted to hire Hareidim. The site included no advertisements which the ultra-Orthodox community could find distasteful or against their values. This site not only brought thousands of job opening to this community's attention, but it also removed a major concern that Hareidim have when they apply for jobs – rejection simply because of who they are: Hareidim. I met with young ultra-Orthodox males who described the fear they usually experienced when walking into job interviews - they knew there was a good chance the employer would reject them simply because of their clothing and background. On this site, the employers are saying, "I want you," and this made the process much easier for the Hareidim who were looking for jobs. The regular All Jobs site includes a charge to become a full member with all the services of the site, including assistance with writing a resume and professional preparation for job interviews. We recognized that most Hareidim would not pay this membership due to their poverty, and because culturally, they are not accustomed to paying for this type of assistance. To solve this problem, we raised money – primarily through the Leo Jolsen Parnassa Project – to provide Hareidim with free memberships to "All Jobs for Hareidim." That offer along with a massive advertising campaign led to hundreds of Haredim becoming members, making use of the full range of All Jobs services.

*With Yeshua Meshi Zavav of ZAKA and Avraham Kop of*
*Ezras Achim, two ultra-Orthodox leaders, discussing*
*the benefits of employment in their community*

Another project of our taskforce was to help establish an internal Hareidi employment service. Many in the ultra-Orthodox community would never go to a source outside the community for assistance of this kind and many don't have the Internet access required to find the "All Jobs" site. Our internal service utilizes Whatsapp on cellphones, and uses representatives within the Hareidi community who find ways to advertise available jobs. This service has also assisted hundreds of Hareidim to find jobs.

One of the most rewarding moments of the 19th Knesset when a young ultra-Orthodox male came to the Knesset to thank me for helping him find a job. He said that he worked for a month and then a huge amount of money was put into his bank account! He described how good it felt to have the ability to buy his children food and clothing. Hearing his words and seeing his face was incredibly rewarding and satisfying for me on a personal level.

This project enabled me to work in close contact with some of the movers and shakers within the Israeli ultra-Orthodox community. I will write more in a later chapter about some of the personal challenges I faced and continue to face regarding my relationship with the ultra-Orthodox community. This particular project, however, reflects the disconnect between public statements against me which emanate from that community and the quiet, behind the scenes work and deep, positive relationships which I have established with many in the Hareidi community in recent years.

Aside from helping poor families leave a life of poverty, helping Hareidim enter the workforce led to an additional and extremely meaningful result. CEO's whom we convinced to hire Hareidim have reported about the unity which has resulted from hiring these new employees. Ultra-Orthodox young men are, for the first time in their lives, meeting secular Israelis and are discovering that despite the difference in lifestyle, secular Israelis are wonderful, value-centered people. This runs counter to what they have been taught throughout their lives about the secular community. And it works the other way as well. Secular Israelis are getting to meet and develop relationships with Hareidim, and are learning that these are fantastic, family-oriented young men, many of whom have been quietly involved with community service for years. This runs counter to their image of the ultra-Orthodox community which has been colored by pictures of extremists protesting or even being violent and by ultra-Orthodox political leaders screaming horrible things about secular society from the Knesset podium. Neither of these images reflect mainstream ultra-Orthodox society and both sides are learning that they can be friends and even share happy family occasions together. This was an unexpected and an incredibly uplifting by-product of the efforts of this taskforce. Despite currently not serving in an official Knesset capacity, I continue to manage these projects and am dedicated to their continued success.

A second taskforce which I established was a lobby for renewable energy and energy efficiency. This taskforce presented a report to the Knesset which demonstrates that if the government chooses to invest in this realm, Israel could reach a goal of obtaining 80% of its energy from clean, renewable sources by 2040. These sources include solar, wind, and wave energy. It is a difficult decision for a government to make since we have limited budget resources and so many pressing needs in welfare, education and health, and because of the high percentage of our budget that goes to defense. Nevertheless, we held meetings with Finance Minister Yair Lapid and other officials in the Finance Ministry, and engaged Energy Minister Silvan Shalom in serious discussions on the issue. We also served as a source of pressure on the government to reach its stated goal of 10% renewable energy by 2020.

In the middle of the term, MK Eitan Cabel asked me to take over as head of the lobby for preventing the suffering of animals in the Knesset. We held a few events during which we discussed how we, as a country, can do an even better job in this area. We also presented awards to activists who demonstrated care and professionalism in exposing and confronting companies that do not adhere to relatively strict Israeli laws against animal abuse. This was an area of activity which broke down political barriers in the Knesset. Members from almost every party showed an interest in getting involved in our efforts, and this also enabled me to work closely with a wide range of MK's. I am thrilled that my colleague and friend, MK Yael German, has taken over the chair of this lobby for the 20th Knesset along with MK Itzik Shmuly and I continue to be intimately involved in the planning and activity of this taskforce.

*Visiting the shelter of "Live and Let Live" animal welfare organization*

A fourth taskforce brought the Meatless Monday project to the Knesset cafeteria. Towards the beginning of my Knesset term, I met with Miki Haimovich, one of the most popular news anchors in Israel. Since retiring from television, Miki has dedicated herself to educating Israelis about the impact of meat consumption on our health, on the environment and on the animal population. Research indicates that 18% of greenhouse gas emissions result from the production of meat and huge amounts of water are used.

*The kickoff event for Meatless Monday in the Knesset cafeteria along*
*with (l to r): Knesset Director General Ronen Plaut, Miki Haimovich,*
*Speaker Yuli Edelstein, MK Amir Peretz, Justice Minister Tzipi Livni*

Meatless Monday does not suggest that people should become vegetarians but rather, that people should try to refrain from eating meat for one day per week. Evidence has shown that just one day without meat can drastically improve our health, can have significant impact on the environment and it no doubt demonstrates compassion to animals. Thanks to our efforts, the Knesset became the first parliament in the world to bring Meatless Monday to its cafeterias. This does not mean that no meat is served, but that many more vegetarian options are offered.

The kickoff event for this Knesset project included the Knesset Speaker and many MK's from across the political spectrum, with many expressing support and even committing to forego eating meat themselves for one day per week. The prime minister was not able to attend the event, but made a public statement that he was accepting this upon himself, as well. The impact of these efforts can be seen in the Israeli public. Twenty-five percent of the Israeli population reports that they have cut down on the amount of meat which they consume.

I also chose to head three other taskforces, mostly to raise awareness both among the Israeli public and in the halls of government. Lobbies for dialogue between the secular and ultra-Orthodox communities, inspiring more immigration to Israel from North American Jewry, and to promote organ donation in Israel all touched upon issues close to my heart. These lobbies led to increased discussion, debate, and awareness regarding these important issues.

# DIPLOMACY

My decision to run for Knesset related to my desire to improve our country internally. I wanted to deal with issues related to the ultra-Orthodox community, religion and state, and unifying around core Jewish values. I never imagined that I would play any role in diplomatic efforts. Former MK Yochanan Plesner (current president of the Israel Democracy Institute) pulled me aside one day before our inauguration and told me that he thinks I could play an important role in the Knesset's diplomatic efforts. He explained that aside from being head and shoulders above the other MK's in my ability to communicate in English, the fact that I have a Western mind which understands the Western world gives me another advantage. He added that, in his opinion, the fact that I was a religious rabbi was a third, important element which I brought to the table. Plesner added: "There will be criticism of the fact that you travel a lot, but it will be a one-day news story and the good that you can do for our country will far outweigh the one negative news story about your travels."

I took this charge very seriously and decided to make this a focus of my work in the Knesset. My first official role came when I was appointed chairman of the Knesset delegation to the South African parliament. I studied the history of Israel and South Africa and quickly learned that there was absolutely no relationship between the parliaments of the two countries. I met with past and current ambassadors as well as other Foreign Ministry officials to gain an understanding of what I could do to improve this non-existent relationship. There was a consensus among the experts with whom I met that there was nothing that I could do to reignite a parliament-to-parliament relationship between the two countries, but that if and when Nelson Mandela would pass away, that would create a window of opportunity to improve the situation. They said that I must make sure to travel to South Africa to pay my respects to this great leader and that such an act of respect could open a door for me into the South African parliament.

Nelson Mandela died on December 5, 2013. As soon as plans for his funeral were announced, the Knesset contacted me and told me that I would be flying to South Africa along with the prime minister and the president. A short while later, the Prime Minister's Office announced that the prime minister would not be attending. Some theorized that this was because Netanyahu did not want to be criticized for the high cost to the Israeli taxpayer of such a flight and foreign visit. Others said that the prime minister feared a very public cold reception at the memorial service. I was then told to prepare for a flight with President Peres. Then, however, the President's Office announced that he was not feeling well and would not be making the trip. Many believe that once the issue of the high cost was raised by the Prime Minister's Office, the President's Office feared the same criticism. Regardless of the reason, I was told that in the end, Israel would not be sending a delegation to the memorial service since the delay caused by all the back and forth led to their being no more commercial flights to South Africa in time for the funeral.

Knesset Speaker Yuli Edelstein felt that not having an Israeli delegation to this event would have very negative ramifications for Israel and his office stepped in to try to find a solution. They asked five other MK's to quickly pack and be prepared for the trip. It took a few hours, but they found a small plane which they could charter to South Africa. After some negotiations with various ministries regarding how to divide the cost of the trip, we were told to head to the airport. We waited for quite some time at the airport because of two major problems: 1) We did not have permission to fly over African airspace. 2) This tiny jet needed to land somewhere to refuel along the way and we did not have approval to do so from any of the countries along the route. Time was becoming an issue, so the moment we received permission to fly through Egyptian airspace we rushed onto the plane and the rest would be figured out once we were in the air.

While in the air, we received permission to land and refuel in Djibouti. But since they are not too fond of Israel, we were prohibited not only from deplaning, but we also could not look outside the place. We had to make sure that all our window shades were closed so they would not even need to lay eyes on an Israeli! Upon hearing this I questioned how we could trust them to safely refuel our plane. The answer? Not to worry, French soldiers would be there to make sure all was secure....

Thank God, we landed safely in Johannesburg, and, already late for the start of the service, we were rushed to the packed stadium which hosted the World Cup final in 2010. We were seated in a section set aside for members of parliament from around the world and this was an opportunity to network and meet MP's, mostly from Europe. When the announcer welcomed the Israeli delegation, mistakenly saying that the delegation was led by Prime Minister Netanyahu and President Shimon Peres, there was a warm applause, similar to that of other delegations. The crowd was swaying to music throughout the ceremony and, after a few hours, I felt caught up in the rhythm and swayed along.

This visit, exactly as predicted by the experts, paved the way for an official visit to South Africa half a year later.

Thanks to the work of Israeli ambassador to South Africa, Arthur Lenk, I was welcomed into the parliament by the ruling African National Congress party, and had a productive meeting during which I made a formal request for renewed parliament-to-parliament relations between our countries.

The meeting, on the heels of Operation Protective Edge, had its tense and difficult moments, but as I told them while defending Israel's actions in Gaza, the most important thing is that we are talking to one another. I also met with leaders of other parties, including some that are extremely favorable towards Israel, and was able to establish close relationships with a handful of MP's. Aside from visiting parliament, I was truly inspired by my visit to Robbins Island, where Mandela was imprisoned for 18 out of his 27 years in jail; and my tour of Liliesleaf, where Mandela and others planned their clandestine efforts against the government, and where many – including Jews who were assisting them – were arrested. That visit yielded contacts with whom I have been in touch when issues of concern such as BDS-related activity have arisen. I am proud to have played a role in making this important breakthrough.

The Knesset named me to the official delegations to the European Union parliament and to NATO. This responsibility placed me in meetings with visiting parliamentary delegations from nearly every country in Europe. The MP's generally criticized us for "settlement construction," and I always directed the conversation back to history and the establishment of the PLO before there were any settlements. While most of the meetings revolved around the Israeli-Palestinian conflict, I always steered the discussions to other issues such as technology and renewable energies. These responsibilities also brought me to Europe where I met with MP's from across the political spectrum. I quickly learned some tools for effective diplomacy.

*Making the case for Israel with members of the French parliament*

*Engaged in public dialogue together with MK Nachman Shai*

*with members of the German Budenstag*

*Presenting to members of the Canadian parliament*

Being willing to acknowledge that Israel has issues that it must deal with and not sweeping our challenges under the rug was an important dynamic in diplomatic give and take. I also learned that the small talk between us, the non-political and non-diplomatic conversations, were almost as important as the policy and political discussions.

British Ambassador to Israel, Matthew Gould, came to meet with me one day and said that MK Isaac Herzog cannot continue to effectively carry out his position as head of the Israeli parliamentary delegation to the UK parliament while serving as head of the opposition. Ambassador Gould asked me if I would co-chair this delegation along with my good friend MK Hilik Bar.

Hilik and I became friends while traveling to Nelson Mandela's funeral and during an official Knesset visit to Washington and New York. I gladly accepted this additional position and looked forward to working with Hilik to improve the critical relationship between the Knesset and the UK parliament. I did manage to make one trip to the UK parliament to begin the process of improving those relations, but Israel went to elections before we could take any meaningful action on this front.

I found that my most important and impactful diplomatic work took place through my participation in the Knesset Christian Allies Caucus. While we are losing friends and support in various governments and parliaments around the world, there is growing support for Israel among Christian members of parliament on a few continents. If we cultivate relationships with them, we can make huge progress for Israel on the international scene. They can have a massive impact on their own parliaments and governments as well as in the United Nations. This is an area where my upbringing in the United States and understanding of Christianity, along with my rabbinic ordination and religious background, was of major assistance.

*Father Gabriel Nadaff, a Christian leader in Israel*

These MP's love Israel because of its spiritual dimension and they want to hear about it and talk about it on that level. One of my visits to Capitol Hill was for a celebration of the reunification of Jerusalem, and Christian members of Congress told me straight out how thrilled they were to hear a Knesset member quote the Bible and speak about the spiritual importance of Jerusalem. I, of course, welcomed members from this caucus whenever they visited Israel and, again, focused on the spiritual and biblical dimension of what they were experiencing in Israel. Among the many highlights of my trips for the Christian Allied Caucus, the most memorable was walking into an arena in Hungary - the country which from which my grandmother, may she live and be well, was transported to Auschwitz - and seeing over 10,000 people waving Israeli flags and singing Hebrew songs in support of Israel and the Jewish people.

My meetings in the Knesset with members of Congress and parliaments from around the world were quite routine, but there is one moment which sticks out. I was meeting with a senior member of the Hungarian parliament and we were about to finish and pose for a photo shoot, when he suddenly said to me, through a translator: "There is a terrible law which the Knesset has been dealing with to ban foie gras from being sold in Israel."

Without giving me a chance to cut in and comment, and without knowing that I was the MK who sponsored the law, he continued to explain how the geese are fed in a very humane way, and he even said, "I want you to come and visit and see how the geese line up to be fed because they enjoy it so much."

I told him that this was apparently his lucky day since I am the MK who proposed the law. I added that all the evidence I saw indicates that this is the worst possible animal torture and that the process goes against our value system. He again invited me to come to Hungary to see the process with my own eyes and the meeting ended in awkward fashion, to say the least.

The trip which had the most impact on me, personally, with no connection to its diplomatic component, was my participation in the Knesset delegation to Auschwitz to commemorate 70 years since its liberation. There are many moments that I will never forget from that trip. The first was the flight, itself. Just being on a flight for a few hours with Knesset members and ministers from across the political spectrum yielded some fantastic conversations – some small talk and some quite political. The second was the moment I walked out of the plane and felt the piercing cold of that January day in Poland. I have experienced cold winters in my life but never anything on this level. Third, I truly enjoyed seeing Polish police closing off intersections to enable this Israeli delegation to make its way towards its destination. And, finally, there was the camp, itself. I walked everywhere proudly holding the commentary on the Bible written by my great-grandfather, Rabbi Elimelech Fischman, who was exterminated there in May 1944. It was surrealistic to walk along that train platform, stopping at the spot where just seventy years ago Mengele sent my relatives to their death, but with our group surrounded on all sides by the Knesset guard in their dress uniforms, proudly holding Israeli flags. It helped me to continue to internalize that we live in the most magnificent of times where the impossible is possible.

That night, we had a joint parliamentary session with members of the Polish parliament. I was fascinated as MP after MP stood up and explained to us that Poland is not to blame for what happened on their land during World War II and that they hoped we did not hold this against them. We used the session and the emotions the MP's expressed to push them to fight against anti-Semitism in their country and throughout Europe, as well as to pressure them to demonstrate even greater support for Israel.

The frustrating component to my diplomatic efforts and involvement was the lack of strategy and teamwork regarding Israeli foreign policy. Similar to the issue I raised in the chapter about my committee work concerning the lack of a plan for Israel advocacy, I felt that everyone involved was doing their own thing when it came to diplomacy. The Knesset foreign relations department did an excellent job in preparing MK's for their meetings in the Knesset and for overseas visits, but there was never a feeling of being part of an overall strategy and plan from the highest levels of government on down. I believe this hurts us in our diplomatic efforts and hope that this changes as quickly as possible.

Former MK Plesner was right. A news story did emerge about MK's who traveled the most, and I was in second place on the list. Being second and not first meant that I was not the focus of the story. Fortunately, the fact that I was the MK with the highest attendance and voting record mitigated any possible criticism. Yes, I traveled quite a bit, but my trips were quick and focused, and I always made sure to be back in Israel to carry out my responsibilities inside the Knesset as an MK.

**Meeting with Maryland Governor Martin O'Malley**

*Speaking to New York City legislators at City Hall*

*Marching down Fifth Avenue at the Celebrate Israel*
*parade with NYC Mayor Bill de Blasio*

*Sharing an iftar dinner with moderate Arab leaders*

*and our host U.S Ambassador Dan Shapiro*

# LIFE AS AN MK

Serving as a member of Knesset is most certainly a great honor but it is also a position of great responsibility. I wanted to do the best job possible, and, in order to do so, I had to first develop a top-level staff. Each MK is given two staff members. By comparison, members of the House of Representatives have between 16 and 18 staff members.

*Visiting one of my closest friends on Capitol Hill, Rep. Doug Lamborn*

On one of my visits to Washington, I sat down in my hotel room after spending time in the offices of several Congressmen, and was able to divide the responsibilities of my staff of two into close to ten full time positions that I saw in each of the congressional offices. Therefore, my staff needed be first rate. They had to be dedicated and we had to be a team.

I was very fortunate to have two volunteers with me throughout the election campaign and the three of us jelled into a team. It was only natural then for us to continue to work together in the Knesset. I named Alisa Coleman, a neighbor from Bet Shemesh, as my chief of staff, and Benjy Goldberg, an Israeli from an English-speaking home with an American mother, as my spokesman and legislative assistant. Due to the high volume of English speakers who I knew would turn to our office, and to also deal with the English-speaking press, it was critical for me to have a staff which could communicate in English. I also needed someone who understood Israeli culture. Benjy was the perfect blend, and the combination of Benjy and Alisa created the "dream team."

*A true team: with Benjy and Alisa (and extended family)*

We made a joint decision that every e-mail addressed to me (as opposed to great numbers of e-mails that are sent to all MK's as a group) would be answered. Our office was bombarded with e-mails, largely, but not entirely, from English-speakers, who finally had an address in the Knesset to which they could send their problems, concerns, or questions - and actually receive an answer! Nothing made me prouder than meeting strangers on the street who thanked me for my office's assistance in helping them solve a crisis or navigate through Israel's difficult and complex bureaucracy.

We also decided that we would hold open hours for people to come and meet with me in the Knesset. Having interned in the U.S. Congress, I saw the importance of constituent relations and it was obvious to me that this included meetings with "constituents." I put that word in quotes because we did not represent any specific regions and I actually had no official constituents. I met with all kinds of people without knowing or caring whether they voted for my party. The Knesset does not meet on Sundays, so this became our day for what came to be known as "Congressman Hours." We dedicated specific hours and people made appointments to meet with me for 10-15 minutes. I was quite stunned when I found out I was the only member of Knesset who was holding weekly meetings of this kind. The issues raised in these meetings were quite varied and, aside from being able to aid people with their struggles and needs, I thoroughly enjoyed that personal contact with such a wide range of citizens.

*Running in the Jerusalem Marathon with MK's*
*Nachman Shai and Danny Danon*

*Demonstrating for Jonthan Pollard's release outside Secretary*
*of State John Kerry's hotel along with MK Hilik Bar*

*President Shimon Peres at a Jerusalem Day celebration*

The Knesset also does not meet on Thursdays, so we decided to use this day for visits all over the country. During these tours I came in contact with many incredible citizens who are working to make our world and our state a better place. I was especially inspired by the organizations that are dedicated to helping special-needs children. I can honestly say that I came home from every Thursday visit with renewed motivation to do my part in making our country a better place for its citizens.

Sundays and Thursdays were also the days to work on writing legislation, preparing for the week's agenda including planning for committees and writing speeches. They were also the perfect time to sit with my staff and reflect on how we have been doing and what we can do better. I often timed my overseas trips from late Wednesday night through early Monday morning thus enabling me to fulfill my work obligations abroad for a few days while still managing to be back in time for all Knesset activity.

Benjy, my spokesman, was responsible for helping me deal with the press. A Knesset member must have a continued presence in the media because this is generally the only way in which citizens know what is being accomplished. As we were told in our pre-Knesset orientations, if we do something good and it is not in the press, it is as if we didn't do it. But I quickly learned that one cannot think that way. In actuality, the satisfaction of helping people and doing good work is the greatest reward we can possibly derive. The press is inundated with material from politicians, there is limited space for stories from the Knesset, and this leads to a daily battle among the spokesmen for coverage. Unfortunately, many Knesset staffers resort to leaking information to reporters in exchange for coverage of their MK. I refused to be part of that "game," and was happy that Benjy had no interest in breaking that code of ethics. If it meant less coverage in the press (which it did), so be it. The press also prefers the more sensational, controversial, and negative stories over positive, feel good ones. There were MK's who pulled stunts or said controversial things for the sake of having their names in the newspapers and for face-time on the prime time news. Again, we would have no part of that.

A perfect example came in the wake of the murder of the three boys who were kidnapped in Gush Etzion. I went around the Knesset and convinced MK's from all parties with Jews (including my good friend, MK Dov Henin from Hadash) to study mishnayot in memory of the three boys. We divided up the entire Seder Nezikin (the Order of Mishna which deals with damages) and completed it in time for the Shloshim commemoration, 30 days after the boys were buried. Benjy sent this story of unity among MK's to the press outlets. Sadly, no one printed it.

Despite the challenge, Benjy did a masterful job getting press coverage for much of what we were doing. I enjoyed the challenge of being interviewed and generally had a good rapport with reporters.

*Speaking at Memorial Day commemoration at a military*
*cemetery in Afula and attempting to share words of comfort with*
*a grieving mother of a son killed in the Yom Kippur War*

The biggest challenge was in dealing with the ultra-Orthodox press. My goal was to keep my cool despite the fact that they were generally on the attack and quite negative towards me and my party. I calmly explained our goals – giving all Hareidi young men a general education and a chance to support their families with dignity, for the ultra-Orthodox community to be a part of Israeli society, and for a more moderate approach to religion and state in order to enable broader Israel to embrace and be proud of their Judaism. They seemed to relish having me on their shows so that they could beat up on me. I actually valued the air time that enabled me to share my message.

For me, the most memorable and poignant moment on Hareidi media came during one of my interviews on the prime-time show on "Kol Chai," the most popular ultra-Orthodox radio station. The host asked me how I, as a religious rabbi, could possibly suggest that young men should leave rabbinic seminaries to join the workforce. I asked for his permission to read a few sentences from Maimonides and proceeded to simply read: "Anyone who chooses to study Torah and forces others to support him (which is what is happening in the current system with the government using taxpayer money to support these young, married man in their religious studies) has brought shame to God, disgraces the Torah and loses his portion in the world to come." There was a pause from the host, and then he said, "You are quoting Maimonides from like one thousand years ago? How is that relevant today?"

This was an amazing moment which showed me that there are classic sources which support my side of the argument. Jews have always viewed working and supporting families as a value. There was always a concept of a few, select individuals with great intellect in each generation who were deemed worthy of being supported by the community to enable them to focus on study alone. Everyone else was expected to balance Torah study along with work. Knowing that the sources and our tradition sided with what we were trying to do enabled me to deal with the negativity and the attacks which came from the ultra-Orthodox leadership and media.

What also helped me through the negativity was the quiet support which I received from the ultra-Orthodox community. Young, ultra-Orthodox men and women reached out to me on a regular basis and urged me to press forward with our mission, because giving their children a general education and making it worth their while to go to work would save their children from a life of poverty. They also told me that teaching their children that they could balance being religious while pursuing their other interests and dreams would keep them religiously observant. In addition, there were rabbinic figures in the community who expressed quiet support, as well, including one who met with me in my home and said that Yesh Atid was "saving the Hareidi community from itself." When I asked him why he would not go outside and say this publically, he replied that his sons would be thrown out of school and his daughters would not be able to find a suitable young men to marry. Knowing that I had this quiet support made a huge difference for me and enabled me to tune out the noise of negativity.

On a family level there were major adjustments that needed to be made to accommodate life as a member of Knesset. The negativity, especially from the Hareidi press and MK's, led to prank calls on our home phone and people calling and saying nasty things to my children about their father. People would also bother my wife about my politics when she was out shopping. We decided that it would be best for her to tell people to e-mail me with any questions, concerns or criticisms instead of placing her in the difficult position of having to defend me. The issue of shopping was actually a major change for me since I used to enjoy doing the family shopping. This ceased once I entered the Knesset because there was no such thing as a quick run to the market. The endless stream of people that would stop me to talk to me either about politics or to seek my assistance with personal needs made it difficult for me to shop for the family. A similar issue arose while attending Synagogue on Shabbat. Well-meaning people saw me and, with no malice at all, spoke to me about politics. However, I really needed a break from politics on Shabbat so I began to pray at a nearby yeshiva instead of at the community synagogue.

Knesset life took its toll on our family routine. Prior to serving in the Knesset, I was home for supper nearly every night and available to help my children with their homework, as well. The Knesset schedule, including party or political events in the evenings, changed this dynamic. I learned to treasure Shabbat and the quality family time it provided. I still found ways to involve myself with homework, projects and other activities, but it took planning and complicated time management. The position required quite a bit of travel and we had numerous "white nights" including two times that I slept in my Knesset office. We did, however, establish a rhythm which included driving my children to school every day that I was home. It helped me to jumpstart my schedule knowing that I had those few precious minutes with them before the craziness of the day began.

There was one element of serving as an MK which no orientation or consultations could have prepared me for. We woke up on the morning of June 12, 2014 to find out that three boys were missing. Nothing was the same from that point onward as we lived through the 18 days until, tragically, the boys' bodies were discovered, followed by Operation Protective Edge. As public figures, we were called upon to be part of both the public healing and also the very private acts of comforting and consoling families that were living through the worst of tragedies.

*Participating in a Knesset prayer service for the three missing boys*

While, on the one hand, seeing this suffering in an up close and personal manner was devastating, these families and soldiers inspired me and filled me with hope for our collective futures.

The families of the three boys, and especially the mothers, found a way to elevate their suffering above politics and thus they unified our nation. When they announced the unity rally while the boys were still missing I was so afraid that the event would be a failure and actually was against it. Rabin Square in Tel Aviv is the site where massive demonstrations take place. When the Israeli left wants to flex its muscles, tens of thousands fill that venue, just like when the Israeli right wants to make a show of force. When Maccabi Tel Aviv wins the European Cup, tens of thousands celebrate there. Would people actually attend a night of prayer and singing for the missing boys?

I was back stage with the mothers before the rally and they kept asking if people were filling the square. To my great surprise and delight, a massive crowd showed up and the mothers rallied the country that night. The families already knew that the outlook wasn't great, but they held on to any glimmer of hope. I will never forget when one of the mothers turned to Health Minister Yael German that night and said, "It was so hot outside today. Do you think they are giving the boys enough to drink?" That touched me so deeply. This was a mother who, on the one hand was rallying an entire country to unity, and on the other hand simply worrying about her son.

*At the rally with the Sheyer, Frenkel and Yifrach families*

Sitting at the funeral for the boys just a few days later, and looking at those three young bodies wrapped in Israeli flags, I remember saying a prayer that I hoped this would be the worst funeral I would ever have to experience. Little did I know that the next few weeks would bring me to the most painful of funerals. The war began and our schedules as Knesset members changed from committees, votes, meetings, and interviews to visiting injured soldiers in the hospital, attending funerals and houses of mourning, and even visiting the soldiers on the Gaza border.

Before we went to lift the spirits of the soldiers near Gaza, I asked my spokesman, Benjy, what I could bring the soldiers. Friends and family in Silver Spring, Maryland, my hometown, raised $1,000 for the soldiers and I wanted to use these donations to do something special for the soldiers along the frontlines. Benjy told me that we should bring them ice cream. I laughed, not believing what I just heard. He wanted me to come to these brave warriors with ice cream? Benjy said to me, "You asked me, a former soldier, what you should bring. I am telling you that you have to bring them ice cream." So, we ordered $1,000 worth of ice cream from Ben and Jerry's in Kiryat Malachi. They super froze the cups, and we made our way towards the Gaza border. I entered bunkers with the ice cream and those brave warriors morphed into little kids.

They were so excited to get their ice cream cup and their faces lit up with joy as they enjoyed every last drop. They then expressed their appreciation to the people who donated the ice cream. They were surprised that people in Maryland were thinking about them and were inspired by the fact that they were fighting not just for their state but for the entire Jewish people.

I will never forget going into a hospital and being handed a list of the wounded soldiers who were being treated there. We visited the soldiers who were "lightly injured" since soldiers with worse injuries were generally undergoing surgery and other critical care. I walked into one of the rooms and sitting there was a 21 year-old who lost his left hand. He was downgraded to "lightly" injured because there was no imminent threat to his life. I asked him if there was something I could do for him (the silly things that come out of our mouths….). He replied, "You can get the doctors to fix me up so I can return to fight with my unit as quickly as possible." Yes, they are young boys who love Ben and Jerry's ice cream, yet they are also brave fighters with the greatest sense of brotherhood I have ever seen.

The funerals were devastating. The sounds of the wailing of orphaned children and young widows haunts me to this day. The worst of the worst was seeing glassy-eyed and near-fainting fiancées. At one point I walked up to a grieving mother after one of the funerals and blurted out the cliché that we have been trained to say: "I am sorry for your loss." The mother looked at me and said, "Sorry? I am not sorry for my loss. I am devastated and we will mourn for the rest of our lives. But I am not sorry. I am proud that my son died defending the state of Israel and the Jewish people." What a statement! What a perspective! We truly are a remarkable nation.

The inspiration rose to a higher level when two lone soldiers were killed. We, in the Knesset, got word that Sean Carmeli from Texas was killed and that his friends feared that very few people would attend his funeral which was called for 11:00p.m. in Haifa. I stood at the Knesset podium and called upon everyone watching on Knesset TV to try to attend. Even more significantly, the call which made the biggest impact came from the Maccabi Haifa soccer team. The word spread via social media that Sean was a devoted fan of the team and people should come to the funeral. That night, 20,000 people attended Sean's funeral. Had I not been a Knesset member who got through with the help of police, I would not have been able to make it into the cemetery. The ramps from the highways were clogged with cars. It was an amazingly powerful experience.

The next day I was told that Max Steinberg from California was killed. Aside from making another call to the public to attend his funeral, I was put in contact with Max's parents who would be coming to Israel for the first time. I gave them a sense of what would be happening in Israel and what to expect during the funeral while trying to find the right words to comfort them. They asked me to eulogize Max during the service, a request that touched me deeply. I did my best to give honor to a special young man whom I never met. Over 30,000 people braved the summer heat and came to pay respect to Max. We received reports that the people on the overstuffed busses and trains making their way to the Mount Herzl Military Cemetery sang the Israeli national anthem and other songs of hope and inspiration.

Attending these two funerals and seeing first-hand how the families were comforted and even uplifted by the national embrace which they received, enabled me to emerge from these devastating experiences with hope and optimism for our nation's future. Seeing this side of our people in such an up close and personal manner throughout the war was the most inspiring aspect of being an MK and, I believe, actually transformed me as an Israeli, as a Jew, and as a person.

*Delivering a eulogy for Max Steinberg, of blessed memory*

*Mourning with Max's family and friends after his burial*

# EPILOGUE

I served in the Knesset for two years. While I am proud of both my party and myself for what we were able to accomplish during that brief period of time, it was far too short. Yesh Atid was founded and I became involved in politics in order to get things done. The party continues to work towards those goals from the opposition and I continue to work towards them from outside the Knesset. But this is mostly a time to be a strong opposition party and develop into THE alternative to the governing coalition. I continue to be very involved in what is happening in the Knesset and look forward to returning as a member of Knesset and continuing to change the country for the better through legislation, taskforces, committee work, diplomacy, and using the position as a platform to help lead our country.

Even when we return to power, I believe that the current system of government needs transformation in order to allow significant change to occur in our country. There must be more accountability for members of Knesset, and direct elections for regional representatives will go a long way towards achieving that goal. I worked on this issue while serving in the 19th Knesset, and there is an existing plan which should be implemented that divides the country into 60 regions. It allows for 60 seats on a national level and 60 based on these regions. I hope to make this concept a focus of mine when I return to the Knesset. In addition, we need to find a way to create stability for governments so that ministers know that they have many years to enact reforms and long-term plans can be brought to fruition. So many of the issues which I worked on in the Knesset – the environment, public health, conversion and ultra-Orthodox education and employment – require a perspective which projects beyond just two to three years of governing. I hope to work towards the creation of a professional, non-political committee to analyze and spearhead change in this realm. Government stability and MK accountability will create an entirely new political reality and substantive change can finally be realized.

Serving as the first native English-speaking member of Knesset in 30 years was an additional honor, and it transcended simply serving as an MK. I am thrilled that I have been able to continue holding Knesset office hours for English speakers during the 20<sup>th</sup> Knesset as well. We have a long way to go to smooth out the many issues and challenges which face English-speaking immigrants, and I look forward to returning to the Knesset to continue the path we started from the inside.

However, this doesn't have to be me, alone. We are a significant immigrant group both in numbers and abilities. We need to stand up and have our voices heard even more than we do today. We have so much to contribute to Israel and if we simply muster the courage to speak our broken Hebrew – grammatical mistakes included – and dare to immerse ourselves in a culture which is foreign to us but not impossible to navigate, we can do it in all realms – school boards, companies, municipal government, religious councils and national politics.

I will continue to do my part in trying to lead our country on a path towards having more tolerance and respect as we unite around core Jewish values and as we strive to fulfill our destiny as a light unto the nations. I invite you to join me in this effort and have no doubt that through our collective effort we can turn this dream into a reality.

# APPENDIX – SPEECHES

# Inaugural Address – February 12, 2013

Eight years ago, my wife and I took our four children, hugged our parents, said goodbye to all our friends and family, and boarded a flight full of new olim from the United States, chartered by Nefesh B'Nefesh. We took our seats, and the captain began to describe the flight plan in detail. At the end of his speech, he said: "Rest, relax, and enjoy the flight. I'm taking you home."

I'm taking you home. After 2,000 years of exile, we were on our way home to the Land of Israel, to the State of Israel.

We arrived with a Zionist spirit and with the hope of a better Jewish life. We decided to leave the United States, choosing instead to be part of the Jewish Zionist project, the State of Israel. We found an amazing and unique country, but it is impossible to ignore the problems we face here in our homeland.

Some 70 years ago, my grandmother, Mrs. Ethel Kleinman, may she live and be well, emerged from the death camp of Auschwitz and began a new life together with my grandfather, of blessed memory, whose brother, my Uncle Zvi, is with us here today in this chamber.

With a lot of hard work and no shortage of miracles, the two of them managed to established a beautiful, upstanding family.

My grandmother told me that there were no sectoral divisions in the death camps. Nobody spoke of hiloni [secular], traditional, religious, or haredi [Ultra-Orthodox].

The Nazis, may their names be blotted out, did not attribute any significance to semantic differences between the groups.

As far as they were concerned, they were all Jews, subject to the same cruel fate. In our darkest and most painful hour as a people, we demonstrated the ability to be unified.

I am disheartened that now, precisely when we have returned to the Land of Israel, there is not enough unity, and each sector takes care of itself without considering the collective good.

When I fought in Beit Shemesh for the rights and safety of all its residents, I suffered curses; I was spat upon, stoned, and even received death threats. These all hurt, but what hurt the most was the knowledge that this was coming from other Jews. I also experienced success when we bonded together – from secularist to ultra- Orthodox – as when we worked on the massive protest in Beit Shemesh last year. There I shouted out loud that the time had come to tear down the walls we have built between us, to reunite, and to work together to improve our future as a society, a state, and a people.

The Yesh Atid Party and its head, Yair Lapid, have taken the important and courageous step of not merely understanding that the time had come to unite and break up the sectoral partisanship that characterizes Israeli society and politics, but also that the time had come to take real action. I am proud to stand here as a rabbi, a haredi, and a Knesset member from the Yesh Atid Party.

I must, first of all, thank my wife, Dina, for her support during all of my public activism during recent years, which included a lot of time out of the house, and my children: Shlomo, Devora, Chaya Miriam and Zahava.

I also wish to thank my mother, Leah Lipman Zeiger, who made aliya a few months ago, and her husband, Alan Zeiger. Without your help and support, I would not be standing here today.

It is hard for me to believe that I am standing here without my father, judge Ron Lipman of blessed memory, who passed away eight years ago.

Yet I sense my father, I know that he is with me every day. His personal example accompanies me and guides me, especially in my participation in Yesh Atid.

My father served as a federal judge in the United States. He knew how to combine Torah study with serving his country and the Jewish people. He showed the beauty and the unifying force of a religious lifestyle integrated with work and society, all while observing a Judaism characterized by moderation and mutual respect.

I must emphasize that this was not my father's invention. This was the way of Judaism throughout history. The Torah itself commands us to work for six days a week. A medieval Jewish text, Sefer Mitzvot Ha-gadol, states that this is one of the 613 commandments – to go to work and provide for your family. The Mishna teaches us that "any Torah that is not accompanied by a trade will result in idleness and cause sin," and the Talmud instructs us that "a father must teach his son a craft." Maimonides teaches us that one who decides to study Torah and saddle others with the responsibility of providing for him desecrates God's name and "has no share in the world to come."

The classic legal code Shulchan Arukh explicitly teaches that every morning one must pray, study Torah, and then go to work.

My father thus followed in our tradition of combining Torah and work. The time has come for us, the members of the Knesset of Israel, to help restore this value to our land.

Torah students should not be impoverished their whole lives.

They should study Torah, provide for their families comfortably, and thus cause a sanctification of God's name in the State of Israel.

Regarding equal service for all, when several tribes of ancient Israel wished to remain on the East Bank of the Jordan River and not enter into the Land of Israel to fight alongside the rest of the people, Moses, our teacher, replied: "Will your brothers go to war while you sit here?" We are all familiar with, and identify with, the principle that "all of Israel is responsible for one another."

We need not demand that every yeshiva student serve in the IDF.

There will also be civil service programs in hospitals, with Magen David Adom, in neighborhood patrols, and providing assistance to Holocaust survivors – mitzvot and admirable actions that no rabbi can say oppose Torah values.

Everyone, including yeshiva students, must contribute to the country through civil or military service. I am proud to be a Knesset member from a party whose leader has a vision, who understands that the time has come to restore the true Jewish tradition of combining Torah with work.

As a rabbi and an alumnus of haredi yeshivot, I wish to utilize this opportunity to address my haredi brothers and sisters personally and directly: There is no us and them. There are no two sides. We are brothers.

We are all Jews. With this belief in mind, we must cooperate and work together to bridge the gaps between us. I want to make a request of my haredi brothers and sisters: Look your children in the eyes. You know that most of them are not really suited for studying Torah day and night for their whole lives.

I and tens of thousands of other haredim in the United States studied in yeshivot and attended universities.

There is no contradiction between the two. Not only did this not harm our Torah study – it reinforced the Torah. We learned that it is possible to remain students of the Torah, Torah scholars, haredim – literally, "who tremble" at the word of God, but also prepared for the job market and ready to provide for our families comfortably.

As an educator, I am proud to be Knesset member from a party that champions revolutionizing the educational system and bringing us back to being world leaders in education.

As a relatively new immigrant, it is painful for me to see fellow olim who are not getting what they deserve. I was a counselor in the former Soviet Union during the '90s, and I saw people who suffered simply because they are Jews. How can it be that the same people immigrated to Israel and now suffer because they are not halachically Jews, despite the fact that they are from Jewish lineage? We must allow them to convert with dignity, and we can even do so in accordance within Orthodox Halacha.

When I was a yeshiva student and olim from Ethiopia began to arrive with Operation Solomon, I volunteered with them every day.

I saw the fire in their eyes during their first days in Israel. It pains me to see how they suffer from discrimination and racism, which, to my great chagrin, I see every day in my hometown of Beit Shemesh. I intend to work on legislation that will banish discrimination and racism against both Jews and non-Jews.

It pains me to see hard-working army veterans and young couples who cannot afford to buy a home.

Tens of thousands of housing units are being constructed in the hills of Ramat Beit Shemesh, but the natives of the city and the grandchildren of its founders cannot afford to buy homes there.

The time has come for the state to help them buy homes.

I am proud to be a Knesset member from the Yesh Atid Party, a party that identifies with everything I have mentioned, and that has risen up to address the problems in Israeli society – including what I have already noted as well as changing the system of government, support for small businesses, decreasing the cost of living, fighting against religious coercion, and most of all, creating real unity within the nation. Our success as a nation and a state will result only from our unity, in both the spiritual and the practical sense.

Moreover, I am proud to be the Knesset representative of hundreds of thousands of olim from English speaking countries, who deserve adequate representation. As a former citizen of the United States, I intend to work to advance the connection of Diaspora Jewry with the nation that dwells in Zion.

I opened these words with a lesson from my grandmother, and I will conclude with another lesson of hers. When I called her to tell her that we were making aliya, I readied myself for anger and sadness about the fact that we were taking her great-grandchildren to the other side of the world. I was in for a surprise. Instead of getting angry, she recited the words of the shehecheyanu blessing: "Who has kept us alive, sustained us, and brought us to this occasion."

She explained, "When we were on the boat from Europe to the United States, I asked myself how could it be that we were not going to the Land of Israel? Now, you are realizing my greatest dream."

It is easy to forget that building the State of Israel, in which we all take part, is the realization of the dream. As King David put it: "A song of ascents: When God returned the exiles of Zion, we were as dreamers."

As a relatively new immigrant, I still sense the greatness of the realization of this dream. The time has come to return this Zionist spirit to every citizen of Israel.

This spirit demands that the entire nation of Israel cooperates and works together to build this state into a world leader in all areas, but on the basis of Jewish values and as a realization of our mission to be a light unto the nations.

As I stand here now, a mere eight years after moving to Israel, as a member of the Knesset of Israel, as a participant in a revolution attempting to change and improve our country and to restore the Zionist spirit to the its citizens, I will follow in my grandmother's footsteps. I, too, will bless God on this momentous event: "Who has kept us alive, sustained us, and brought us to this occasion."

## Speech in the Knesset Plenum prior to voting on legislation to draft the ultra-Orthodox – March 2014

Mr. Speaker. Honored ministers.

I stand here before tomorrow's vote filled with tremendous pride. I stand here as a rabbi with a lot of pride, as a person who observes and Torah and mitzvot, with a lot of pride, as a member of Yesh Atid with a lot of pride, because tomorrow morning I will vote for the law which will lead to equal service for all. The source for that pride comes because of our classic sources and now I will read some sources so we will understand where that pride comes from.

The Mishna in Tractate Sotah Chapter 8 Mishna 7 it says: "In a war of mitzvah, all go out to fight, including a groom and a bride." A groom and a bride, men and women must go out to fight and there is no line in this Mishna which says "Except for." It doesn't say "except for those who…" All go out to fight.

So the question is what is a "war of mitzvah?" Are we fighting now in a "war of mitzvah?" So I open Mainomides and Maimonides in Mishna Torah in Laws of Kings Chapter 5 asks: "What is a war of mitzvah?" It is wonderful that he asks the question for us. So, what is a war of mitzvah? He says a few things and now for the quote: "Helping Israel from an enemy that comes upon them." We can all agree that we live in a period of time and in a situation in which we have enemies all around us who want to destroy us and to throw us out of here. "From an enemy that come upon them." And in a war of mitzvah, ALL must go out to fight at it said in the Mishna.

The Torah says over and over again "those that go out to fight in the army of Israel," "those who go out to fight in the army of Israel." We serve! When I sit and talk with chareidim and appear in the chareidi media, they ask me how I can say what I say. "How are you, a rabbi, saying this? Did you forget that there is the tribe of Levi? The tribe of Levi didn't serve in the army. And, therefore, we the chareidi population we are the tribe of Levi today and we don't have to serve even if it is a war of mitzvah." The basis for this claim is also in Maimonides in the Laws of Shemita and Yovel Chapter 13. Maimonides explains what is the tribe of Levi - by the way, the tribe of Levi served for the nation in the Tabernacle and in the Temple. They did serve the nation! They were a part of the broader society. But it says in law 13 "and not the tribe of Levi alone." And they say "we see from this that it is not limited to the actual tribe of Levi. And they say to me – chareidim who I meet with and in their media – that everyone can define himself as being in the category of the tribe of Levi. And, we, in the chareidi population, today, we are the tribe of Levi." But listen to what Maimonides says. "Not the tribe of Levi alone but any person from anywhere in the world whose spirit comes upon him and he understands on his own to separare to stand before God to serve him." That person can claim to be like the tribe of Levi. Not that he is taught from first grade that his role is to do nothing but learning Torah. But someone who on his own feels that he is capable of learning day and night. He can be one of those few special people in each generation who can claim to be like the tribe of Levi.

I want to remind you of the dispute in Tractate Berachot between Rabbi Shimon bar Yochai and Rabbi Yishmael. Rabbi Shimon bar Yochai says that he decided to do nothing else but learn Torah. Rabbi Yishmael said this is not correct. You have to study Torah and do other things including supporting your families. And it says in the Talmud "many did like Rabbi Yishmael" – combining Torah with other things – "and they succeeded." They saw success. "Like Rabbi Shimon bar Yochai" - many tried to act like Rabbi Shimon bar Yochai" – "and they were unsuccessful." Because we are talking about a select few in each generation – as we recognize in the law that we are voting on tomorrow – they are truly capable of studying Torah day and night and this is all that they want to do in their lives. As an alumnus of chareidi yeshivas, I remember what happened. We learned for many hours. But those who truly learned day and night and did not do anything else? We are talking about select individuals. So to suggest that there is a population with 50,000 who are like the tribe of Levi, this is simply not the situation according to all of our sources.

And I want to say something else. "Torato Umanuto" – "Torah is his trade" – this is that they learn all day and there are commentators who say they don't even have to pray because they learn Torah day and night they don't do anything else. Can we really say that the 50,000 do nothing else? I don't know. When I leave the Knesset at night and go to fill up with gas at the station at the city exit, there is a restaurant there called Halo Taiman. And it is full. Full with yeshiva students. And it is ok. It is really ok. They can go to eat and enjoy. But to claim that they are in the category of "Torah is his trade?" That there only desire is to study Torah? This is simply not correct. And we are talking about a distortion. And that is s shame. Because they are taking a concept - "Torah is his trade" – something which should be for those who are truly representing the nation, and they are claiming that for everyone, and suddenly there is no respect for Torah. They are misusing this term and, in my opinion, this leads to disgracing the Torah instead of bringing honor to the Torah.

It is important to emphasize that in our law there is chareidi employment. Close to 30,000 young men will be able to go out and join the workforce, to sustain their families with dignity. The Mishna says "any Torah which is not accompanied by work, in the end it will be nullified and leads to sin." I will repeat that "it will be nullified." The Torah, about which the Chareidi MK's always say they say we have to fight for the Torah, if there is no livelihood, the Torah is nullified according to the Mishna. It is nullified! You, and I am talking to their empty chairs now, are fighting for something which leads to the nullifying of Torah, and we are fighting to preserve the Torah.

The Talmud teaches that a father must teach his son a trade. They must have a trade. And under the chupah every groom accepts upon himself to support his family. And it says in the Shulchan Aruch – the Chareidi MK's always stand and claim that "we follow the Shulchan Aruch." What does it say there? In Orach Chayim 156:1 that after praying in the morning and studying Torah "he should go to his business." The Shulchan Aruch says in black and white - "afterwards he should go to his business." So no one should say we are destroying something. We are strengthening the Torah. We are strengthening our tradition. And that is why I said that I stand here with pride saying that I am going to vote for the law.

I have pride to be part of the Yesh Atid party. In less than a year we have made progress on our flag issues – the law to reduce the number of ministers which we voted on this morning, the equality in service law which we will pass tomorrow morning, the overhaul in education led by our Education Minister, in less than a year. "We have come to make change" is not just a slogan. Really. This is what we are doing.

A chareidi rabbi sat in my apartment and said "Dov, keep going. You will save us from ourselves." And this is what we will do. I sat with young chareidi men from Bnei Brak and they said to me "we want to serve, our enemies all around us want to destroy us." And we will give them the ability to serve. And I truly feel that we will preserve the beauty of our tradition and on the beauty of our Torah.

I want to conclude with what I believe is truly missing. And before I finish I want to thank Minister Peri for the work that you did and to MK Ofer Shelach for your work. You are our pride how you were so dedicated to passing this law.

What is missing is that in chareidi yeshiva even when they study Torah, they don't join with us in prayer. As a young child in the United States in a synagogue with chareidi congregants, every Shabbat we stood together and prayed. I call from here, that even with we have disagreements, we can all agree that right now soldiers are out there right now fighting to defend us and to give the yeshiva students the ability to study Torah. So, let's go – secular, religious Zionists, traditional, and chareidim – let us pray together on behalf of the soldiers and if we do this, this will demonstrate that we are truly on nation.

He Who blessed our forefathers Abraham, Isaac and Jacob - may He bless the fighters of the Israel Defense Force, who stand guard over our land and the cities of our God from the border of the Lebanon to the desert of Egypt, and from the Great Sea unto the approach of the Aravah, on the land, in the air, and on the sea.

May Hashem cause the enemies who rise up against us to be struck down before them. May the Holy One, Blessed is He, preserve and rescue our fighting men from every trouble and distress and from every plague and illness, and may He send blessing and success in their every endeavor.

May He lead our enemies under their sway and may He grant them salvation and crown them with victory. And may there be fulfilled for them the verse: For it is Hashem, your God, Who goes with you to battle your enemies for you to save you. Now let us all respond together – all of the Jewish nation together – Amen. Thank you.

# Speech in the plenum about ultra-Orthodox employment and education – February 2014

Mr. Speaker, honored minister, member of Knesset

I stand here as an alumnus of ultra-Orthodox seminaries and the chairman of the lobby to assist the ultra-Orthodox population with integration into the workforce. I will focus on a part of the Taub report that relates to the ultra-Orthodox population. A week ago I visited the Taub Center and sat with Dan Ben-David and was given an explanation of the report. I recommend that all Knesset members really go over this report to really understand the true data.

The report made me happy. There is no discrimination against the ultra-Orthodox in the labor market. However, there is a need for them to have an academic degree. This is what the data shows. Of course, there is always room for improvement but the ball is truly in the court of the haredi public.

Here are the statistics:

Among haredi men with an academic degree 71% find work as opposed to those who don't have an academic degree in which just 34% find work.

Among women it is 76% versus 50%.

In terms of salary, it is important to listen to this.

Men with an academic degree earn 80% more than those without a degree. And the average wage. What is the average wage? 13,500 shekel per month. Thatis the average salary of those with a degree.

Husband and wife, if they both have an academic degree – they earn 157% more than those without an academic degree.

With regard to degrees – for haredi men between the ages of 25 and 44, fewer than 8% have an academic degree. You can do the math here about how many have an academic degree and why they are not in the labor force.

Matriculation exams – only 5% earn a matriculation certificate.

In the report they write that there is an increase of more than 60% in the numbers studying in the rabbinic seminaries and I welcome this. We want young people to studying Torah but there is no reason why they should be studying in rabbinic seminary and in parallel to study for a degree in higher education. There is no evidence at all that in Yeshiva Chaim Berlin or at Torah Vadaat in New York or in Ner Yisrael in Baltimore that they are not Talmudic scholars on the same level as those in rabbinic seminaries here in Israel and they take a few hours each week to learn towards a degree.

They should study in rabbinic seminaries. But this is not enough.

The bottom line, Mr. Speaker, and I conclude with this point. The ultra-Orthodox want to break out of the cycle of poverty and there is one way to do this.

From this Knesset podium I call on the ultra-Orthodox Knesset members and I call on the rabbis: cooperate with us. We don't want people to be poor. So we need that in ultra-Orthodox schools they should teach math, English – basic general studies. Demand that in the ultra-Orthodox high schools they take two hours a day to study in order to study towards earning a matriculation certificate. Establish rabbinic seminaries with programs of higher education – not co-ed, everything in the spirit of Torah. Produce Talmudic scholars, full-fledged haredim, with a degree that will help them support their families with dignity.

This is good for the ultra-Orthodox population. This is good for the Torah of Israel. And this is good for the State of Israel.

Thank you.

# Speech in Knesset Plenum about Jonathan Pollard – March 2013

On November 21, 1985 I was a ninth grader in Silver Spring, Maryland. Just 30 minutes away, at the Israeli embassy, Jonathan Pollard was arrested, under suspicion that he spied for Israel. I recall my thoughts as a young American Jew. It bothered me very much that Jonathan was arrested for spying for an ally of the United States. My father, Judge Ron Lipman, of blessed memory, explained to me that Jonathan broke the law and people who break the law must pay the price for doing so.

I do not stand here as someone who wants to push aside a crime that anyone committed. However, the time has come to recognize that Jonathan has paid the price. Yes, he spied. Yes, he violated American law and for that he rightfully went to jail. But as his health continues to deteriorate and the list of American leaders calling for Jonathan to be released including Lawrence Korb who was assistant secretary of Defense at the time of Jonathan's arrest, continues to grow, it has become clear that Jonathan has served his time and it's time for him to be freed.

A few weeks ago, I stood up in the United States Embassy in Tel Aviv and renounced my American citizenship as required by Israeli law as a condition for serving in the Knesset. I confess before you that it was an emotional experience for me and I even shed some tears. I had trouble saying the words that the clerk asked me to repeat. Why was it so difficult? Because so much of who I, at least, strive to be - tolerant, fair, understanding, and compassionate – was inculcated in me by the United States of America. I cried because my words felt like a rejection of those strong American values which I was taught by my parents and teachers.

That 14 year old American boy who struggled with the arrest of a fellow Jew, but grew to understand Jonathan's arrest and verdict, stands here today, close to 28 years later, as a member of the Israeli Knesset. I planned on using the distinguished platform of the Israeli parliament, to address our friend, President Obama, in English. However, I learned that, unfortunately, that is forbidden according to the Knesset by-laws. Therefore, I will address President Obama in Hebrew.

Mr. President. In the name of my colleagues in the Knesset, and in the name of the citizens of Israel, I ask you to please not let Jonathan pass away in prison. Please act with the American values of compassion and tolerance and free Jonathan Pollard. Please reflect on the shared biblical values of our two nations along with the close relationship and friendship between our two countries - both which you have championed as President. Please enable Jonathan who has paid the price for his crime and has suffered enough, to live the remaining years of his life in freedom.

In conclusion, I have a request for all my fellow members of Knesset and all fellow Jews. We must pray. Please join me in beginning every day with a prayer to God for Heavenly mercy to help us succeed in freeing Jonathan. In the merit of the prayers of the Jewish nation on a daily basis, with God's help we will see Jonathan with us in the near future. Thank you.

# Protocol of the session and vote on legislation forbidding men who receive to give their wives a divorce the right to stay in the religious section of the jail – November 26, 2014

**Deputy Speaker Penina Tamanu-Shata:** We move now to the "Law of Rabbinic Courts - Restrictions on Get Refusers" who are Incarcerated of Knesset Member Dov Lipman. The brief explanation will be from the side microphone and the person who will respond in the name of the Justice Minister will be Minister Silvan Shalom. MK Lipman, please.

**Dov Lipman (Yesh Atid):** Mrs. Speaker, honored ministers, members of Knesset

**Deputy Speaker Penina Tamanu-Shata:** Members of Knesset. Members of Knesset. Please remain quiet. Member of Knesset Amnon Cohen please. Thank you.

**Dov Lipman (Yesh Atid):** All of us most certainly share a goal to reach a situation where there are no agunot in the State of Israel, and we have the tools to accomplish this. We are talking about legislation which forbids those who are called "get (divorce document) refusers" – they are in prison, they are in jail, but they sit and their lives are very comfortable in the Torah branch of jail. It is forbidden to give men who refuse to listen to the decision of a religious court that they must give their wives a divorce to claim that they are religious and thereby allow them to sit in the Torah branch of jail. Therefore, we are making it forbidden for them to be in the Torah division of jail. This will put pressure on them and this also sends an important message: They cannot claim to be religious. The law also forbids them to be in contact with people outside of jail who can encourage them to continue on and bring suffering to their wives. They can only be in contact with their lawyers, and only with their relatives, and for a limited period of time. I call upon all Knesset members to vote "in favor" so we can take one small step forward towards reaching a situation in which there are zero agunot. I want to thank Deputy

Minister of Religious Affairs Rabbi Eli Ben Dahan for his support and his assistance in moving forward with the legislative process. Thank you.

**Deputy Speaker Penina Tamanu-Shata:** Thank you Knesset Member Lipman. Minister Silvan Shalom please come up to answer in the name of the Justice Minister. After that we will move on to a vote.

**Minister of National Infrastructure, Energy and Water Silvan Shalom:** Mrs. Speaker, thank you. Knesset Secretary, Knesset members, government ministers.

The "Law of Rabbinic Courts 5755 - 1995" from this point and on "The Law of fulfilling court decisions" allows the rabbinic courts to issue restrictive orders for a man or woman who refuses to fulfill a rabbinic decision for divorce, from this point and onward "the refuser." These orders are part of the various sanctions placed on the refuser with the goal to force them to heed the court and give or receive a divorce, including imprisonment. The law even permits the rabbinic court to restrict certain rights given to prisoners in order to lead to the point that the refuser will heed the decision of the court. The legislation which is before us seeks to widen the list of prisoner rights that the court can rescind: 1)Telephone calls with the exception of phone calls with an attorney or an immediate relative as long as the length of these calls with family members do not exceed ten minutes 2)Staying in the Torah branch of jail 3)Receiving food with the "mehadrin" kosher certification.

The phenomenon of divorce refusers, unilaterally chaining a man or women by a spouse, is a very difficult one. Therefore, we must act against it using all possible legal means including imprisonment for refusing to listen to the decision of the religious court.

This legislation works in consonance with the existing law because imprisonment, according to line three of the law of fulfilling court decisions is civil imprisonment whose goal is to force the person to listen to the decision of the religious court and is not a means of punishment.

Therefore, the keys are in the hands of the refusers to be freed from imprisonment if they agree to a divorce.

It is important to note that passage of the legislation must include, by obligation, looking at the complexities involved and we must pay attention to the consequences if they exist.

Therefore, the government stance is to support the legislation in its original reading and afterwards the law will move forward in consonance with the Public Security Ministry and the Justice Ministry.

Do you agree? Agree.

**Deputy Speaker Penina Tamanu-Shata:** Thank you to the minister. There is agreement from the bill's sponsor.

We are moving on to a vote on the law of rabbinic courts – adjustment to restrictions for divorce refusers who are imprisoned 5774-2014 in its original reading. Knesset members you are asked to take your seats and please vote "in favor" or "against."

39 members of Knesset are in favor of the legislation. Zero are against it. The committee with jurisdiction over this legislation is the Law and Justice Committee and the legislation will move to this committee.

## One Minute Speech in the Knesset Plenum about rabbis and women immersing in the mikva during conversion – December 2, 2014

Mr. Speaker, distinguished Minister,

A week ago I read a story about a young woman named Jennifer and then I called her and she related to me how she reached the end of her conversion process and when it came time for the immersion in the mikva, by mistake, and I want to emphasize that it was my mistake, the rabbinic judges entered the room while she stood there naked. She explained the shame that she felt. I spoke to her in a bit greater depth and then I also spoke with other women who went through conversions. They explained how after they have gone through the entire conversion process during which there was an emphasis on the laws and the value of modesty, and they accepted this upon themselves, it is so difficult and unpleasant to even be in the same room with the rabbinic judges when they immerse, even if they see nothing.

I started to research the issue in our texts, and I found, to my great surprise, that there are halachic decisions from Rabbi Uziel, from Rabbi Shmuel Salant, and even from Rabbi Moshe Feinstein, who say that despite the fact that the ideal is that the immersion be done with the rabbinic judges in the room, in a time of need it is possible for women to immerse without the judges in the room.

Therefore, I sent a letter to the deputy minister of religion in which I requested and demanded that we continue with the policy that the judges are in the room without looking as the official policy but that we give the option to women who want it that they can immerse without men in the room. This is okay according to Halacha and it removes this entire problem from the conversion process. I hope that the deputy minister of religion will accept my suggestion and that all women will feel at peace and enjoy when they reach the climax of the conversion process when they immerse in the mikva. Thank you.

# Speech in Knesset plenum about Judaism and Christianity – May 13, 2014

Good afternoon Mr. Speaker, distinguished minister, honored Knesset and guests.

In our history as the Jewish people, there is a long list of countries, of leaders, and people who caused us suffering and pain. But at a certain point, they changed their ways. Despite the great difficulty, we must find the way to forgive and to look forward.

In the story of the Jewish nation with the Christian Church, one leader stood up, Pope John XXIII, who not only requested forgiveness for the dark past of the Christians towards the Jews, but he also did something courageous. During World War II he saved thousands of Jews from extermination as a liason for the Pope in Turkey and Greece. After his appointment to the position of Pope in 1938 he hosted a delegation of American Jews in the Vatican and said, as the distinguished Speaker mentioned, "I am Joseph your brother." The words that Joseph the righteous, the son of Jacob, our father, to his brothers in Egypt when he revealed to them that he is Joseph and wanted a new, fresh start of love and friendship between them.

Pope John XXIII worked to change the Church prayer book and to remove any negative word towards the Jews. Despite the fact that he died before the end of the Second Vatican Council, John XXIII raised the issue of the Church's relationship with Judaism and Jews many times. In a document which emerged from the Council, there is nothing short of a revolution regarding Christianity's approach towards us. They invalidated any claim against the Jewish people in any involvement in the death of Jesus. They invalidated any claim that the Jews have been cast off by God and that the Church replaced them. They accepted that there is a covenant between God and the nation of Israel. And they spoke out against anti-Semitism.

We, as the Jewish nation in the Jewish state, must express our gratitude to Pope John XXIII and look forward with regarding to the relationship between us and the Christians in the State of Israel and throughout the world.

I want to explain how it was for me to be a young Jew in America where the majority were Christians. We played basketball together, we cheered for the same sports teams together, we helped each other, and we worked together on the many issues of which we share the same values. It is important to emphasize that I meet many groups of Christian tourists along with members of parliament from all around the world and they are loud supporters of the State of Israel and they are prepared to stand by our side through fire and water. They prove this time after time.

We must make sure that Christians feel at home in the State of Israel and it is our obligation to protect their welfare.

Now that we have built a glorious Jewish state, we must make use of our state as a platform for cooperation with Christians throughout the world to light up the world with values of equality, tolerance, peace, and co-existence. Thank you.

# Speech in Knesset plenum prior to the vote about the foi gras legislation – July 10, 2013

Mr. Speaker, Honored Minister, Distinguished Members of Knesset.

We disagree about many things in this house. There are debates about the burning issues of the time and close votes to determine our direction.

However, we must never forget the things which we agree upon and which can unite us. When we talk about Israel as a Jewish state we must make sure that our values reflect core Jewish and human values as taught to us in the Bible and also as our human instincts dictate to us.

And that is what brings us to today. I am proud that this law received wall to wall support in this house – from ultra-Orthodox to Secular, from Jews to Arabs. All of us can unite and state that we want our country to have nothing to do with the process of fattening goose liver.

Let's remind ourselves what we are talking about here. A farmer takes a goose, sticks a pipe down its throat and forces it to eat and eat and eat. Three times a day over the course of an entire month, the farmer forces food down its throat until its liver explodes to six times its normal weight. This force feeding brings to the goose to a situation in which it has trouble breathing and standing on its own. At that point, the goose is brought to be slaughtered. Can anyone really justify such an action just to make it easier to smooth the goose liver on a cracker?

Our country can be proud that it already banned doing this horrific act within our borders and the time has come for us to have zero business association with this practice.

This is where core human and Jewish values must kick in and we must define what kind of people we are.

As Mahatma Ghandi said, "The greatness of a nation and its moral progress can be judged by the way its animals are treated."

And If I can put my rabbi hat on for a moment, we have a reminder of the importance of treating animals properly every day - twice a day - when we recite kriat shema. We say, "And I will give grass in the fields for your animals, and you will eat and be satisfied."

God says first there is food for the animals and then for humans. The Talmud teaches that we learn an actual law from here that we must feed our animals first and then ourselves so as not to cause suffering to our animals who will see us eating and feel pain that they are not eating.

The law currently says that there is a ban on importing this product and as agreed between myself and Minister Yair Shamir, in committee we will change the language from import to business, making it clear that it will be prohibited to sell this product in Israel.

I thank everyone in this house for their support of this important legislation and am proud that that we as Jews are uniting around this core Jewish value and that we as people of shared values are joining with non-Jewish MK's to pass this law.

With God's help we will be a light unto the nations and other countries will follow suit and together we will rid this horrific practice from the world.

# Speech in the Knesset plenum about air quality in Israel – May 14, 2014

Mr. Speaker, honored minister, distinguished member of Knesset.

"The State of Israel leads the world in public health and care for the environment."

That is what the newspaper headlines must say throughout the world. But, to my great sadness, this is not the situation. Just the opposite. Reality is far from that.

The World Health Organizations report places Israel in 12th place in polluted air. 12th place? How did this happen to us?

It is true, thank God we are living in a state which is developing at a rapid pace and there is a direct correlation between industry and pollution. But, if we would be thinking long term, there are things that can be done to bring us to a situation where we are actually leading the world in this realm.

This is not easy, and it is not inexpensive in the short term, but the eternal nation is not afraid of a long path. We must take action in the area of the environment not only because it is important to us to have a beautiful and clean state but because there is a direct connection between air pollution and our health.

As Hippocrates said: "If you want to learn about the health of a population, test the air that it breathes, the water that it drinks, and the places in which it lives."

In this context, I want to condemn the horrific decision of the Interior Ministry to remove the environmental organizations from the planning committee – something to cry about for generations. And I call on them to reverse this decision and I call on other government forces to pressure the Interior Ministry to do so.

In the book of Devarim chapter 4 it says: "And guard a lot your lives." "A lot." A word that we do not find many times in the Torah.

So, what should we do?

We have learned from Ashkelon, the city with the highest air pollution numbers in Israel because of the Rottenberg power station in the city. Think for a moment, how we could improve the air and the health of Ashkelon residents, and of the entire state, if we increased the amount of energy that we received from renewable energies like solar and wind energy – sources that are completely clean from any pollution.

In Germany, a country without sun like we have in Israel, they already passed 30% of their energy coming from the sun while we, in Israel, are hovering around just 2%.

With a vision for the long term, and with the help of investment and new rules that could allow all citizens to use their rooftops to create solar energy, we can reach much higher levels of clean energy.

All of us benefit from bottles. Apparently the entire world benefits from them – 300 billion bottles uses per year. 300 billion!

Have you ever thought about where they all go after we use them? Have you considered the amount of energy that is necessary, to make them, deliver them, refrigerate them, and to recycle them? All for two minutes of drinking pleasure! Everything needs energy and our energy is currently coming from polluting sources – and we will continue to be in lowly 12th place!

We have what to be proud of – Recycling rates have reached 77.5%. Now we have to strive to reach 100%.

But, even more than that, let's all use the Israeli creation – Soda Stream – and we won't need to use so much plastic, aluminum and glass.

By the way, I want to solute the Knesset for its Green Knesset program which includes a massive reduction in bottle usage – this saves money, is environmentally friendly and helps our health.

My colleagues, when we think and act green, we all benefit.

There is one more thing that every citizen can do to improve the state of our air – to reduce the amount of meat that we eat.

Meat production accounts for 18% of green-house gasses in the world – more than transportation!

25% of Israelis report that they have reduced the amount of meat that they eat. This is excellent. If we continue to reduce the amount of meat that we eat, this will lead to cleaner air and we will save huge amounts of water, and, we will also be healthier.

I am proud that in a month we will introduce Meatless Mondays to the Knesset cafeteria and I call on all ministers and MK's to enjoy the special vegetarian options that will be offered every Monday so that we can do our part to improve the air that we all breathe.

Returning back to the report about air pollution, I call from here to the Israeli government to invest more in future energies – clean and healthy energy sources. I call on the Israeli Police to enforce all crimes related to polluted water, air and ground with an iron fist.

In addition, I turn to all citizens and ask that each one of you find a way to do something to help the environment that we are leaving for our children. Turn off the light when no one is in the room, cut down on unnecessary trips in the car, recycle the newspapers, there is so much that can be done – we just have to have the will.

The solutions for clean air for us and for the next generations are in our hands. We just have to act.

Thank you.

# Memorial Day Speech at Military Section of Rosh Ha'Ayin Cemetery – May 4, 2014

Dear bereaved families, citizens of Israel

I know that the "thank you" is not a consolation and won't bring your loved ones home. But this is still my obligation.

I moved to Israel with my family nearly ten years ago. We came to a spectacular country. But I know that the state of Israel did not come down ready made from the heavens.

It took a lot of work, toil, tears, and sweat to build this diamond of the Jewish people – the State of Israel.

But even more than this, a lot of blood was spilled in order to build our beloved state.

Your sons, daughters, brothers, sisters, fathers, and mothers sacrificed their bodies and souls so that we can live with security in our holy land.

You, the bereaved families, sacrificed that which is the most precious.

All year round, and especially on this day, the nation of Israel embraces you, thanks you, and expresses its gratitude to those who were killed to sanctify God's name and the land.

A few minutes ago, we all stood still for the siren. I want to share a quote with you from a book written by Education Minister Rabbi Shai Piron:

"At the heart of the day, we hear a siren that unifies all of us around silence. We stand, brother next to brother, and we are quiet. Religious and secular, liberals and conservatives, Ashkenazic and Sephardic, and you – the bereaved families.

All stand together for one minute with no explanations. No one uses the tragedy for explanations that are comfortable for him. No one feels the need to explain. We simply experience the pain through the assistance of the siren in one clear moment of spiritual elevation.

We all discover that at times the best explanation is silence."

"A song of ascents when God returns the prisoners of Zion, we were like dreamers." When I was a child in the state of Maryland in the United States, we went a few times to demonstrate opposite the embassy of the Soviet Union – on behalf of the Jews who were stuck there. I vividly remember one of these demonstrations – someone gave me a sign to hold up and on this sign said "Free Yuli Edelstein." We were like dreamers. Today, I sit in the Knesset as a member of the Knesset, and the Speaker of the Knesset is Yuli Edelstein – that prisoner of Zion who I demonstrated for.

The return of the Jewish people to Zion – Jews are coming from the four corners of the Earth. This is a fulfillment of the dream.

The soldiers of the Israel Defense Force, together with all the security services, are the ones who enabled the fulfillment of the dream of the Return to Zion. It is our obligation to work every day to try to make our country better and in doing so we will give honor to the memory of those who have fallen.

The dedication of soul and body of these holy soldiers who were killed with always be in front of our eyes – we will never forget them.

To conclude, I turn to the heavens with a prayer: May the One Who makes peace above, may He make peace upon us and on all of Israel and we say Amen.

May their memories be a blessing.

# Speech at Auschwitz gathering of MKs and MP's In Poland – January 27, 2014

I stand here as a great-grandson coming for the first time to the burial place of my great-grandfather and great-grandmother who came to Auschwitz on the night of the Jewish holiday of Shavuot in May 1944.

Rabbi Elimelech Fischman and his wife, Rebbetzin Yuta Fischman, were slaughtered not far from here on the horrific and awful night, together with many of their children and grandchildren.

I stand here with tears in my eyes. Tears for my grandmother, Ethel Kleinman, may she live and be well, who had to stand and see her parents and siblings taken to the slaughter.

I have tears for my mother who had the opportunity to meet her Grandfather and Grandmother, as well as uncles and aunts, robbed from her – all of them remained on this ground as dust and ashes. Not even one picture remained.

But I also stand here with great pride. I stand here as a member of the Israeli Knesset. And that makes me declare "Am Yisrael Chai" ("The nation of Israel is alive!")

Despite the attempt by the Nazis to destroy us, we established a Jewish and democratic state. Our state is strong and is flourishing, thank God, despite the desire of many of our neighbors to erase us, and despite other states fighting against us.

I am here to give honor to the memory of my loves ones who were murdered and to tell them with pride that they have great-grandchildren and great-grandchildren that are learning the same Torah that they learned, that are fulfilling the same commandments that they fulfilled, and that are living as free Jews in the Holy Land – the land that they yearned for, and turned to in their prayers three times a day as persecuted Jews. This event, is the ultimate honor for them. "Am Yisrael Chai." May their memories be a source of blessing. Thank you.

# Speech at Faith and Ecology Conference in Jerusalem – October 22, 2014

It is an honor to be here today and I applaud you for this conference and your efforts – I do believe that faith and faith based efforts can make a major impact on improving the environment.

A look through the classic Biblical and religious Jewish sources makes it clear that caring for the environment should be one of those core values which helps define any religious society and that must certainly be the case or Israel as the Jewish state.

The Bible relates in Deuteronomy Chapter 20 verses 19 and 20. "When you besiege a city for many days to wage war against it to seize it, do not destroy its trees by swinging an exe against them, for from it you will eat, and you shall not cut it down; is the tree of the field a man that it should enter the siege before you? Only a tree that you know is not a food tree, it you may destroy and cut down, and build a bulwark against the city that makes war with you, until it is conquered."

The Sefer Hachinuch, one of the midieval commentaries who codified the ritual laws of the Bible, explains this command as a mitzvah, a Biblical commandment, that we cannot needlessly destroy trees of any other object in creation.

Maimonides explains that this prohibition includes the needless destruction of food, clothing, and buildings. The Shulchan Aruch, the Code of Jewish Law, which serves as the primary authority for Jewish law, puts specific limits on industry which causes pollution.

In the very beginning of creation, the Torah says that God put Adam in the Garden of Eden "l'ovdah ul'shomrah" – "to work it and to guard it."

Rabbi Joseph Dov Soloveitchik explained that this captures a conflict built into the very essence of the human-Nature relationship.

On the one hand, we are meant to utilize and exploit Nature. Considered the pinnacle of Creation, the world was created for OUR use, to conquer and manipulate. On the other hand, we are merely custodians of a perfect, divinely created world. Adam and Eve were placed in the Garden of Eden to nurture and protect it.

There is a teaching within Jewish tradition which truly captures the importance and significance of caring for the environment dating back to the time of creation: "When God created Adam He took him and showed him all the trees of the Garden of Eden and said to him – 'See my works, how beautiful and praiseworthy they are. Everything that I created, I created for you. Be careful not to spoil or destroy my world for if you do, there will be nobody after you to repair it.'"

According to this teaching, God, Himself, tells Adam not to spoil or destroy the world which He created. This, no doubt was the basis for Rabbi Samson Raphael Hirsch writing that baal tashchit, the biblical command not to needlessly destroy nature, is- and I quote – "the first and most general call of God."

Yes, caring for the environment is a core Jewish value.

Given the fact that our country is only 66 years old, we have much to be proud of in this realm. 1) Israel is ranked as the second highest Cleantech country in the world according to World Wildlife fund.

2) Over 83 percent of Israeli homes use solar energy for hot water, the highest percentage in the world.

3) Israel's reverse osmosis facility in Ashkelon is the world's largest water desalinization plant.

4) Israel treats 92 percent of its wastewater and reuses 75 percent in agriculture, the highest rate in the world.

5) Regarding recycling, Israelis recycle 20 percent more of their plastic bottles than the United States even though we just started the bottle recycling program ten years ago.

6) Israel is the only country that entered the 21 century with a net gain in trees – over the last 50 years over 260 million trees have been planted.

Finally, CO2 emissions are 11.02 per capita, which is half of what it is in the United States. Yes, we have made great strides in our 66 years to reinforce the core Jewish value of concern for the environment.

But we can do so much more and this effort has become a major focus of mine as a member of the Israeli parliament. Sewage and polluted water from chemical plants and at times – chemical waste – is dumped into the sea.

Just to demonstrate the degree of the problem, in the Haifa harbor mercury and other toxic metal, contaminants made the fish not suitable for food. In many kibbutzim and moshavim there are no treatment facilities beyond sedimentation and aeration with sewage simply flowing into the wadis in certain places.

This waste finds its ways into rivers and eventually into the Kineret, aside from contaminating underground aquifers. We must do a better job in monitoring this area. Waste removal is another major issue.

More than 90 percent of Israel's solid waste is buried in landfills, burned in open-air pits or left to rot in garbage dumps throughout the country. When we compare this to Switzerland which buries just 12 percent of its garbage and Japan which burns just 19 percent, we clearly have a long way to go. Open garbage dumps contribute a large amount of toxic matter to the air, breeds flies, rats, and mosquitos, and contaminates underground water supplies.

We must work towards legislative changes in this realm as well. To that end, I sponsored laws to reduce the amount of plastic bags that are used in our supermarkets, a law that addresses overfishing which is destroying our ocean waters, and I even introduced Meatless Monday to the Knesset cafeteria so that decision makers can be aware that 18% of green-house gasses come from meat production and cutting back a little bit can make a big difference.

These are just a few of the areas in which we can improve.

I plan to move forward with a legislative agenda to help improve our environment and call on all parties to rally together in unity to support these bills. I have no doubt that Education Minister Rabbi Shai Piron who shares my passion for a return to core Jewish values will

work to include more environmental education in our schools.

Together, we can all rally around this most basic value and as the source I referenced earlier said, Be careful not to spoil or destroy the beautiful world which God created and especially not our beautiful homeland.

I conclude with a quote from Avot D'Rav Natan – a source for a wealth of spiritual and core Jewish values. This quote should help clarify what the order of priorities should be in a Jewish state: "If you should happen to be holding a sapling in your hand when they tell you the Messiah has arrived, first plant the sapling and then go out to greet the Messiah."

Thank you.